First-Class Teacher

Success Strategies for New Teachers

Edited by the Staff of Canter & Associates

A Publication of Canter & Associates, Inc.

About the Staff at Canter & Associates

Canter & Associates is a leading provider of staff development materials for educators. Many of the more than 100 staff members are former teachers. All share the common goal of wanting to help teachers succeed in the classroom. Our educational development specialists together with the writing and editing staff contributed not only their professional expertise in producing this book but also a special excitement at the thought of "mentoring" new teachers at the beginning of their careers. We hope the enthusiasm of our staff is contagious and that the ideas in this book go a long way in helping you create your ideal classroom.

Staff Writer
Teresa Langness

Editorial Staff
Jacqui Hook
Deborah Kopka
Carol Provisor
Barbara Schadlow
Vic Schneidman
Kathy Winberry

Design
Joyce Vario
Barbara Smiley

©1998 Canter & Associates, Inc.
P.O. Box 2113, Santa Monica, CA 90407-2113
800-262-4347   310-395-3221
www.canter.net

Printed in the United States of America
First Printing September 1998; Revised July 2000
04 03 02 01   5 4 3 2

ISBN 1-57271-033-0

PD4147

What Makes a First-Class Teacher?

"First-class teacher" can mean a teacher facing a classroom for the first time. It can also mean a teacher who embraces the profession with passion, confidence and ingenuity.

You can qualify as a "first-class teacher" in both senses of the word. Just supply the passion and this book will add the strategies and suggestions to help you hone your skills, expand your confidence, use your ingenuity and tap your potential.

We've packed these pages with planning tools to help you survive your first year—and thrive in years to come. We've compiled the solutions, activities and ideas you may need to get through the day, even your *first* day. We've collected insights to help you launch your teaching career with clear vision. Beyond that, we've added a few ideas to help you plot your long-term path of professional growth.

This book has strategies for elementary teachers, middle school teachers and secondary teachers. As you find a technique that applies to your teaching situation, adapt it to fit your personal style.

You need not read and implement all these strategies at once. Use the contents page and topical index to refer to the areas you want to master first and then to address everyday concerns as they arise. Refer to the book as a resource in years to come as you fine-tune your teaching practices.

New teachers tell us that they come to the classroom hoping to inspire children to learn, to make a difference in a child's life, and to help children become their dreams. Let this book guide you on your noble mission. Apply, practice, adapt and refine the strategies you learn. As you perfect the craft of first-class teaching, may you become your dream in the process.

Contents

A Word from a First-Class Teacher

A powerful essay, excerpted below, helped Jenise Jackson win the First-Year Teacher of the Year award in a contest sponsored by the Education Foundation of Yavapai County and the Rotary Clubs of Yavapai County, Arizona.

I was fifteen when a teacher changed my life. She saw something in me that I did not see myself and nurtured a spark that gave me purpose. It's been twenty-five years since that teacher inspired a shy teenager to pursue the dream of writing and teaching. The road has not always been smooth or easy, but without her initial push, becoming a teacher might truly have been the road not taken.

Today, it is my turn to nurture and challenge. As I work with my students each day, I remind myself to stretch beyond the daily teaching routines and recognize and act on the moment of magic: to help a student see and believe that anything is possible. It is such a moment that makes each day of teaching something to look forward to. My best day in this first year of teaching is not a single day but a collection of such moments.

Five years from now, I still see myself in a classroom with students. Hopefully, I'll have a few new teaching tricks up my sleeve as a result of more experience, but I'll still be sharing laughter, teaching curriculum, instilling responsibility and creating excitement about learning.

Teachers, now more than ever, are role models for the next generation. I plan on being one of those role models.

— Jenise Jackson, Fourth Grade Teacher

CHAPTER 1

How to Get to — and Through — the First Days

***"** The first day I didn't know where to pick up my kids. I knew they were outside, but I didn't know how to get there. Then everybody was coming back in and I was going the other way.* **"**

Your job as a teacher begins the moment you find out you have a position. The more "homework" you do before school begins, the better you can battle those first-day butterflies.

Make a list of the things you will do to prepare. You will need to learn about the unique circumstances in your school that will affect your daily schedule, your classroom policies and your method of tapping the school's resources as you plan instruction. You will need to think about how to work with aides, volunteers, parents and colleagues. You will also need to develop materials, design schedules and create a classroom environment that enhances learning from the very beginning.

The success of your first few days and weeks of school may depend on the forethought you have already invested, so this chapter provides some "food for forethought." You'll also find resources and tools to use as you plan and prepare. Because every school's structure and policies differ, no one checklist can cover all the specific information you need to know, but this chapter will help you lay the groundwork for a successful first year.

Ask the Key Questions

What is the most valuable question you can ask as a new teacher? It's the one that occurs to you at any given moment. Your questions may range from "What should I do in case of a medical emergency?" and "How should I meet the district's educational policies?" to "Where is the cafeteria?" Knowing what to expect and feeling familiar with your school and its policies can affect your ability to move smoothly and confidently through your daily agenda, achieve your learning goals with your students and keep your sanity.

Survivors of the first year give this advice: Ask a lot of questions. If your administration has not provided ample information, you may need to find the answers on your own. You'll probably be surprised at how willingly other people will help you. Keep asking questions throughout the year as new issues arise. You will learn a great deal from your own experiences in the classroom, but you can also gain a great deal from the experience of other staff members.

Before school begins, learn where to turn for information. In some schools, the administration assigns a staff member to help each new teacher learn the ropes. In other schools, new teachers may need to seek out informal mentor relationships. In either case, get acquainted as soon as possible and continue to ask for guidance when you need it.

Whom to Ask

- **Principal:** In some schools the principal (or vice principal) provides most of the guidance for beginning teachers. If this is the case at your school, find out when the principal will be available to help. Your administrator may have such a busy schedule that you will need to plan a meeting well in advance.

- **Mentor:** Your administration may assign you a mentor. The mentor will probably meet with you on a regular basis and remain available for questions. The mentor will offer you information, advice and support. The mentor will probably arrange to observe you teaching your class so he or she can offer constructive feedback on your teaching techniques.

- **Department Chair:** In secondary schools, the chair of your department may be a good resource for both curriculum expertise and information about your school.

- **Teacher Buddy:** Regardless of whether or not you meet with an assigned mentor, seek out a teacher "buddy," an experienced and well-respected teacher who can answer your questions and offer you moral support this year and beyond. Many new teachers form a relationship with a teacher at the same grade level or with a teacher teaching in the same department, but a good teacher at another level who has had experience with a class similar to yours could also serve as your buddy.

What to Ask

As you read on, use the checklists provided and jot down any additional questions that occur to you. You may find these topics addressed in the topical index.

Discover Your District Policies and Procedures

Most school districts and schools offer orientations that cover the basics of school district policies. If you do not receive a full orientation by the district, ask your school administrators to explain the school district policies that apply to you. Use the checklists that follow as you go on a fact-finding tour. Before school begins, meet with your principal, assistant principal or department chair and ask any questions not covered in your orientation or in the printed orientation materials.

Set up your own employee file. Include any materials given to you by your administrators. Ask about items you do not receive. Add your notes from orientation meetings. Check off each item below as you obtain it.

Employee File

Do you have your:

☐ Contract.

☐ District employee handbook.

☐ Benefit forms.

☐ District papers relating to your employment and credential.

☐ District-mandated curriculum for your grade level or subject area.

Learn Your Schoolwide Policies and Procedures

Your first day of school may run like clockwork. However, it probably won't unless you know the "clockwork" of your school. When does the tardy bell ring? Will someone collect your roll sheet or your lunch count? What is the process for recess or dismissal? What should you do if you see a student wandering the halls during class time? What areas on the school grounds are off limits to unchaperoned students?

The questions that occur during the first few days and weeks of school may catch you off guard. Use the "School Policies and Procedures Checklist" on the next two pages to make sure you get all the information you can in advance.

Schoolwide Policies and Procedures
Checklist

Schedules

☐ **Daily class (or period) schedule.** Also find out about recesses, special classes, lunch times and period breakouts, if applicable.

☐ **Bell schedule.** Make sure you know what the various bells mean that ring during the day. Some bells may not apply to your class.

☐ **School-year calendar.** Find out the length of each quarter or semester, the vacation dates, holidays and inservice days, and when the school year ends. Ask any questions about how your pay periods relate to the school calendar.

Schoolwide Routines

☐ **Attendance procedures.** Beginning teachers may not realize that public schools receive much of their money based on attendance figures. Check with your mentor or administrator and request specific directions on your school's procedures for taking and recording attendance.

☐ **Drill procedures.** Most schools schedule fire drills or other disaster drills early in the school year. Some schools post maps on the wall of every classroom to show the quickest route out of the building. Find out where you should take your class once they exit the building. Ask whether you will need to anticipate any drills specific to your geographic region, such as earthquake or tornado drills.

☐ **Lunch counts and collecting money.** Procedures vary from school to school, so learn your responsibilities for taking lunch counts and collecting lunch money.

☐ **Assigned duties.** You will probably be assigned one or more duties at the beginning of school. You may supervise the yard, a hallway, the cafeteria, or the area where students get on and off buses. Learn your responsibilities and find out where to station yourself. If possible, observe how an experienced teacher handles these responsibilities.

Physical Spaces and Materials

☐ **Procedures and rules for common areas.** Learn your school's rules and procedures about student use of the yard, library, hallways, lunchroom and bus areas, so you can teach and reinforce them.

☐ **Classroom equipment and supplies.** If your room has no computer, printer, overhead projector or video player, find out how you can check out the equipment you need. Request training if you need it. Ask whether paper will be allocated to you and find out how to order supplies (e.g., pencils, scissors, posterboard). Find out whom to contact if a piece of equipment needs repairs.

☐ **Office machines.** Before school begins you will probably need to use a photocopier. In some schools an aide or an office staff member runs off all copies. If this is not the case in your school, find out how to make copies, and make sure you budget enough time to get copies made. Learn the school policies for using fax machines, phones and e-mail, and for creating a class Web page.

Continued on next page

Continued from previous page

Curriculum and Assessment Policies

☐ **Curriculum guidelines.** Find out the state and district standards for your grade level or subject area (if you did not receive them from the district).

☐ **Report card guidelines and grading policies.** Check with the principal, department chair or another teacher at your grade level.

Behavior Management Policies

☐ **Your schoolwide behavior management plan.** Be sure to ask about policies for monitoring student behavior in common areas outside the classroom.

☐ **The procedure for sending students to the office.** Ask about working with administrators in the case of severe behavioral problems.

Student Support Resources

☐ **English Language Learning (ELL) aides or teachers.** Most schools develop specific procedures for students with language barriers. Find out how many of your students have been identified as needing support for English language acquisition. Learn whether your school offers an ELL program or a bilingual aide.

☐ **Special education teachers.** Many schools "include" or "mainstream" students with special learning needs in the general classroom. Even so, some students may be pulled out to work with a special teacher. Special education needs might include speech and language therapy, adaptive P.E., or remedial reading assistance. Find out whether your classes will include identified students. Ask about your school's policies and procedures.

☐ **School counselors.** Ask the procedure for consulting with a counselor if you have a troubled student or one who exhibits a severe or chronic behavioral problem. Also ask how you might schedule conference time with the student and the counselor.

Emergency Procedures

☐ **Health concerns and accidents.** You will need to get help quickly if a student suddenly becomes ill or has an accident. Yet many schools have an on-site nurse only a few hours each week. Your advance knowledge of what to do could become a critical factor in handling the emergency. Find answers to the questions on the "Health Emergency Procedures" chart in the resource section at the end of this chapter. Post it near your desk for quick reference.

☐ **Student fights or aggressive confrontations.**

Before school starts find out what policy you should follow if violence occurs and whom you should contact to break up a fight or remove a threatening student.

Health Emergency Procedures
Page 36

Map Out Your Curriculum

When your administrators hand you a textbook, curriculum materials and a set of standards and objectives, you need not feel intimidated. Step back and get an overview of the year, then create loose timelines and set your learning goals. Once you do, you may find that the details of daily planning will more easily fall into place.

As you enhance your sense of timing, you will be able to better judge when to modify your lesson plans. If your class seems engrossed in a productive activity or discussion, you may want to continue it beyond the allotted time period. If students doze or act restless, you may want to alter the activity. Remember that your main objective, to foster learning, supersedes the importance of watching the clock. For this reason, you will want to carefully balance the two priorities of sticking with a schedule and honoring your learning goals.

For each subject you teach, take the following steps to chart out your year.

Before school starts:

- Look at the number of units in your textbook or curriculum materials and determine how much time to allow for each unit over the course of the year. Jot down in your plan book when you hope to start each new unit.

- Count the number of chapters within each unit. Determine how much time you can spend on each one. Pencil in the dates when you will probably begin each new chapter in the first unit.

- Determine how much time to allot for the lesson plans that will cover the content in each chapter.

- Jot down the learning activities you will plan within a sample day and within a sample week.

At the end of the first week:

- After the first few days of school, you may feel better able to estimate the length of time needed to complete the activities in your lesson plans. Assess whether you can easily stay on target given the time you allocated for each chapter. Decide whether you need to modify your schedule or lesson plans to meet your district standards and your own standards for learning.

- Begin to factor in daily activities and special events. As you prepare for each new week, you will want to record in your plan book any upcoming school assemblies or other interruptions you should anticipate. Also record announcements you need to make and details you need to handle so you can manage your time efficiently without interrupting the flow of the learning activities.

At the end of the first unit:

- As you near the end of the first unit, assess the effectiveness of your timeline again. Then map out the chapters for the entire semester and pencil the start dates in your plan book. You will feel glad you planned ahead when a student suddenly announces a two-week vacation and asks for work to complete en route. You can tell the student what pages to read and perhaps offer some basic assignments to send along. Since middle schools and high schools especially emphasize grading, students cannot afford to miss out on the content you will cover during such an absence.

At the end of the first semester:

- At the end of the first semester, complete the process for the remainder of the year, penciling in start dates for each chapter. Remember to reflect, weigh priorities and modify your plan as needed.

Prepare Your Lesson Plans

A good day in the classroom begins with an effective lesson plan for each topic you need to cover. A lesson plan generally includes several elements. (See the "Lesson Plan Elements" example on the next two pages.) It can span the course of a class period or you can introduce the elements over several days. A well-thought-out plan can help you accomplish your learning objectives while keeping students excited about the curriculum. The better your planning, the less likely students will be to become bored and disrupt the classroom, and the more likely you will be to feel calm and in control.

As you review your books and materials, consider which elements you might include in your first lesson plans. You need not include every element in every plan. Your approach will vary according to the age of your students, the complexity of the content, and the length of the chapter or unit.

Use the "Lesson Plan Template" worksheet provided in the resource section to write your own detailed lesson plans. Remember that some lesson plans may extend beyond one day.

Lesson Plan Template

Topic: Grade/Subject: Date(s):

Learning Objectives:

Materials:

Procedures:
(Can include any combination of elements such as presentation, individual activity, group work, class discussion, review and assessment.)

Homework Assignment: (if applicable)

Follow-up Activity:

Lesson Plan Template
Page 37

Lesson Plan Elements

Learning Objectives

Your district standards will help you determine your learning goals for each unit. Keep them in mind as you plan effective ways to teach each chapter.

Start by asking what your students need to know and be able to do by the end of the learning process. Consider objectives that relate not only to the content but also to the skills students need to build.

Example:

- Students will understand and be able to explain photosynthesis.

- Students will demonstrate their collaboration skills.

- Students will learn about the scientific process as they observe the growth of plants.

Instructional Strategies

Instruction can take many forms in today's classroom. Rather than lecturing as students listen, you may decide to have students read together in small groups. You may assign projects that lead them to library sources, software or Internet sites. Review your learning objectives and decide the most effective way for students to develop an understanding of the key concepts and relevant details and, where applicable, to develop hypotheses or conclusions. Consider your students' prior understanding of the subject and anticipate ways to help every student feel challenged yet attain the learning objectives.

Whatever elements your instruction includes, strive to bring the content to life. Read Chapter 4, "How to Engage Students in Learning," and then decide how you will incorporate elements such as the following.

- **Anticipatory Set (an activity to build anticipation)**

  Think of an activity or demonstration that will engage your students' interest, make the topic seem more relevant, or give it personal meaning for students. This "anticipatory set" may include a story, a question, a visual aid or some other device.

- **Presentation**

  Decide how you will formally introduce the content students need to learn. You may want to present introductory information to the class or you may want them to present it to each other. You might, for instance, have students read aloud in groups and summarize the information to each other. If you do present orally to the class, remember that many students tune out during long periods of listening. Engage them by involving them in the presentation.

- **Discussion**

  Discuss the essential questions that relate to your learning objectives. Encourage students to think of examples and implications. Challenge them to determine the significance of the information. Read "Learn Involvement Strategies" on page 130 for ideas on how to engage every student in the discussion.

Continued on next page

Continued from previous page

- **Teaching Aids**

  Teaching aids can enhance or reinforce an oral presentation. As you plan your lesson, make a list of the materials you will incorporate, such as reproducibles, visual aids, videos, software, maps and globes, and charts and diagrams.

- **Group Work**

  Research shows that group work can enhance learning. It can enlist every student as a participant rather than as an audience member. Group work can mean simply asking a question and pairing students to discuss the answer, or it can mean setting up long-term projects in which each group member contributes to the learning. For more ideas on how to incorporate group work into a lesson, read page 178, "Teach Cooperative Learning Skills."

- **Application Activity**

  Provide an assignment that helps students internalize, remember and apply the learning. Afterward, debrief the application. For instance, students might role-play a situation or practice a hands-on activity. You can assign either individual work or group work to help students apply the concept.

- **Assessment and Review**

  Few students learn everything the first time it is presented to them. You can often build in ways to assess student knowledge as you implement your lesson plan. The assessment will help you determine the need for review or repetition. Build future lessons on the knowledge base your students developed through this lesson plan. For instance, you might stop and ask students five things they know about the topic, based on the activities so far, and list their responses on the board. Or you might have them write down three questions they can answer about the topic and three questions they cannot answer. Do not limit your assessments to tests and quizzes. For more assessment ideas, read page 143, "Assess for Success."

- **Follow-up Activity**

  Choose follow-up activities that reinforce and sometimes enhance the initial learning objectives. You may assign overnight homework, group work or a long-term project. It may include family activities or library research. For instance, have students interview their parents or neighbors about their first-hand experience as it relates to the topic covered. In a study of the Westward migration, students might interview their parents or friends about a time when they had to leave their hometown and move far away.

Set Up Your Classroom

The organization of your classroom directly affects student behavior and learning. By thoughtfully planning your classroom environment, you can avoid some of the distractions that keep you and your students from functioning as effectively as possible.

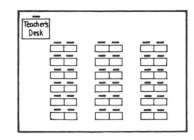

Arrange the Desks

Customize the arrangement you choose for the desks or tables to meet the needs of your classroom and to acknowledge your own teaching style. If you do a lot of work in pairs, arrange the desks in groups of two to four. If you emphasize group discussion, a horseshoe arrangement might help students better see the speaker. The illustrations at the right will give you some ideas. Follow these additional guidelines.

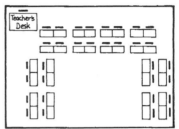

- Make sure all students can see both the board and you from their desks.

- Allow aisle space so you can work with individual students at their desks.

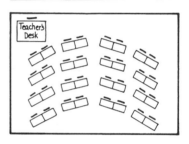

- Create broad pathways so you can easily move around the room when speaking to the class.

- If you plan to conduct cooperative activities, arrange students in small groups.

- Place centers and work-area tables around the perimeter of the room.

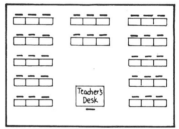

Arrange the Equipment

Find out what special equipment you can access in your classroom. You may have an overhead projector and one or more computers and printers. A portion of the room may serve as a listening center and include a cassette player/recorder. Some classrooms have a TV and a VCR.

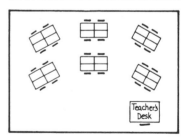

Consider how and when you will use the equipment. You may want to store things out of the way for occasional use, or you may want to set up the equipment now so that students can start using it in the first days of school. Test all equipment before school starts to make sure it works and to see whether you discover any questions about how to operate it.

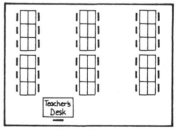

Locate the electrical outlets in your room so you can decide where to store and use the equipment. Remember that the location of computers may depend on how they connect to the printers and to the network.

Sample Seating
Arrangements

Collect, Organize and Store Supplies

Prepare for the school year by stocking up on all the supplies you might need through the year. Find out the procedure for obtaining supplies and ask which supplies you are entitled to request. Before school begins:

- Use the "Supplies Checklist" reproducible in the resource section as you gather your supplies.

- Organize the supplies in labeled containers and store them in cabinets. Use a variety of boxes, cups, baskets. You can also store supplies in hanging shoe bags and transparent boxes.

- Separate the supplies you will distribute to students and keep them on hand.

Supplies Checklist
Page 38

Gather Books and Instructional Materials

Make an inventory of all the books in the classroom. Learn the procedure for obtaining any additional books you need. Many new teachers report that they do not automatically know how to choose among the books and resources available to them. If your school and district allow you to choose among several sources, you may want to spend some time evaluating them and talking with other teachers to see which source materials have proven most effective. Once you decide which combination of books you will use:

- Make student editions ready for distribution. (Find out if there are any record-keeping procedures you must follow when you distribute the books.) Keep teacher editions at your desk.

- Inventory other instructional materials (reading kits, math manipulatives, science supplies, etc.) Find out if it's possible to order additional materials and how you go about ordering.

- Inquire as to whether any hardware or software has been allocated to your classroom. Test the equipment before asking students to use it.

- Set up a class library so students know where to go to find resource materials. You may want to involve students in making small signs for each shelf, to indicate the categories of books in the class library.

- If you have time, shop the flea markets and garage sales for children's books to add to your class library. You can often buy books in bulk for very little if you explain you're a teacher.

Organize Your Files

Because some of your units involve many materials and can extend over days or weeks, you will want to develop a system for storing lesson plans and related materials. Set up a file cabinet with separate sections for each unit. In each section include:

- Lesson plans (including notes about what worked or did not work well).

- Reproducible worksheets and handouts.

- Test keys.

- Ideas and extra materials.

Your first year will probably seem the hardest because you must create your lesson plans from scratch. Filing your materials offers two benefits. You can draw from or add to the files as needed later in the unit. You can also refer to them again next year and refine them as you plan the same unit.

Plan Your Bulletin Boards

Some new teachers feel pressured to prove themselves by putting up elaborate room decorations. Balance the desire for a visually stimulating classroom with the need to save time for your many other planning tasks. You may even want to wait and give students the challenge of decorating the bulletin boards through their first-week projects.

Keep in mind that the bulletin boards should serve an instructional purpose. They usually illustrate a lesson concept or display student work. Consider these tips to make the most of your classroom bulletin board and wall space.

- Use your time efficiently. Before you even begin, plan what will go on each board, take measurements, and gather the materials you'll need. (You might want to check teacher supply stores for bulletin board materials that fit your needs.)

- Plan several bulletin boards or wall areas to display important information for the class (for example: class rules, class jobs, the calendar, schedules and announcements, birthdays).

- Put up a display welcoming the students.

- Prepare one or two bulletin boards with borders and titles, but otherwise leave the boards blank so they can be used to display student work.

- Use a bulletin board to introduce a unit you will be starting soon after school begins.

- You will also find ideas for "First-of-the-Year Bulletin Boards" on the next two pages. These ideas can motivate good behavior, hands-on-learning and a sense of belonging for every student. Refer to those pages to refresh your bulletin board themes later in the year.

First-of-the-Year Bulletin Boards

For Lower Elementary

Hands-On Helpers

- Have each student trace his or her hand on colored paper, cut out the hand and write his or her name on the hand.

- Post all the paper hands on the bulletin board to create a border.

- Keep a Polaroid camera handy. When you notice one student helping another, cleaning up the room, or doing a good deed, snap an instant picture. At the end of each day, tack the photos up on the board. As you fill the board with pictures, you may soon find that everyone wants to lend a hand!

Ace Students

- Reinforce classwide good behavior. Have one group of students drawing a long, curving road or race track on butcher paper. Have another student draw a finish line at the end of the road. Post the butcher paper on a bulletin board.

- Have another student or group of students draw a car (or cut out a magazine photo of a car). Tack the car to starting end of the race track.

- Each time the students have a whole day of good behavior, move the car ahead a little on the race track. Plan a celebration for the day when the car reaches the finish line.

For Upper Elementary

Class Menu

- Label a bulletin board with a sign saying: "Menu: What Room ___ has to offer." Tell students that their classroom offers a unique menu of talents, skills and stories. Let them know that each member of the class changes the flavor or adds an interesting ingredient to the class mix.

- Have students decide on representations of themselves. Each one can think of a unique hobby, talent, interest or aspect of family culture. Students can either draw the objects or bring small items from home. Examples might include a family photo or baby picture, a cut-out magazine picture of the region where the student was born, a favorite recipe, a guitar pick, a baseball card, a poem the student wrote or some other emblem of the student's unique interests or background. Each item or drawing must fit on a paper plate.

- Distribute paper plates to the whole class. Let students affix their representations onto the plates with glue, tape or tacks. Have them sign their names on the plates.

- Help students mount the plates on the bulletin board. Your class display will reflect the uniqueness of each student and provide a springboard for student sharing and for building classroom relationships. You may want to prepare the bulletin board early in the year and keep it up for back-to-school night.

- If you have space below each plate, you can add student work, letting each student choose one completed assignment to post.

For Secondary

Name Your Hero

Older students may enjoy getting to know one another by sharing their heroes. Have students identify a person with qualities they admire. They may each choose among celebrities, public figures, historical characters and even family members. The diversity of the heroes chosen will tell you a lot about your students. It will tell students a lot about one another. Have students create a "Heroes" bulletin board by doing the following.

- Students bring in snapshots, posters, magazine pictures or hand-drawings of their heroes.

- Post all the heroes on the bulletin board. On a separate page, have students write their names, the names of the heroes and a brief statement that tells why they relate to the hero chosen. Post these written statements under the images.

- Hold a class discussion about the traits the students said they admire and about defining what we stand for. Help students understand that while heroes may inspire our goals and dreams, we can each think and act for ourselves and fulfill our own unique potential.

You will probably want to keep the bulletin board up for a month or more. During that time, look for opportunities to revisit the theme as your content dictates. For instance:

History: Have students analyze the traits of historical figures and describe the traits they would define as heroic.

Language Arts: You may conduct a similar analysis of characters in literature.

Science: As extra credit, have students give book reports on biographies of scientists. Discuss heroic traits they portrayed. Students may want to add the scientists to the bulletin board.

Foreign language: Students can translate the names of their heroes into the language they are learning. They can also add heroes from the countries where the language is spoken.

Make Your First Day a Great Day

You have already assembled your materials, arranged the desks and equipment, and put up bulletin boards. Now you must prepare your first day's lesson plans and gather the materials necessary to teach the lessons. Remember three rules of thumb on that first day:

- Make it fun.

- Plan down to the minute.

- Then overplan.

Prepare for more activities than you will probably accomplish on the first day. There's nothing worse than having a lesson that takes much less time than you anticipated, and then not knowing how to fill the remaining minutes. Make sure you include time to teach students about the procedures you expect them to follow. For instruction on how to teach procedures, see page 56. Meanwhile, use the "Suggested First-Day Activities" reproducible in the resource section to plan your agenda.

Make Final Preparations

Conduct a final check of your classroom and of your plans for the day. Take care of those last-minute specifics that will help the school year start smoothly. Remember, you want to project an attitude to students that says, "You can depend on me." Because of all the planning and organization you have done, you can face the day with confidence and a sense of control.

- Review your lesson plans for the day.

- Review your behavior management plan. (See Chapter 2, "How to Manage Behavior.")

- Review your schedule for the day. Check that the class schedule is posted. Make sure you know what duties you have and where to go for any duties.

- Run off copies of all reproducible materials you will need. Organize them so they are ready to distribute.

- Prepare all name tags or desk tags. (You may choose to have students make their own desk tags from the "Desk Tag" reproducible provided in the resource section.)

- Prepare student supplies for distribution.

- Conduct a final check of your room arrangement.

- Post your name and room number outside your classroom and write it on the chalkboard.

Suggested First-Day Activities
Page 39

Desk Tag
Page 40

Offer Warm First-Day Greetings

You build a solid foundation for the entire school year on the strength and warmth you project on the first day of school. Think carefully about the first words you will say to your students. Early elementary students may enter the classroom with their parents on the first day. Take this opportunity to meet the parents and answer their questions. The rapport you build with both students and parents at the beginning can make a difference all year long. (For more ideas, read Chapter 3, "How to Involve Parents.")

Whether students enter the classroom alone or not, greet everyone at the door and introduce yourself. Ask each person's name and repeat it so you will remember it. Above all, welcome every student with a smile. Show that you are looking forward to getting to know each of them. Once your students have found their seats and you begin speaking to the group, tell them a little about yourself and put them at ease. Share your enthusiasm for the projects you have planned for the year. Keep your energy level high throughout the first day so students go home with positive expectations about the new school year.

Adhere to Your Schedule

You will begin to establish habits and routines on the first day. Try to ascertain how long it takes to complete each function as you follow through with the introductions, activities, record-keeping tasks, transitions, and periods of instruction on your agenda. Setting a schedule and following it will help you plan your time realistically and effectively in the days to come. The professionalism with which you plan and organize this day will also set the tone for students' expectations and attitudes.

Size Up Your Day

At the end of the day, reflect on your successes. Ask:

- Did I do everything I planned to do? If there are lessons I didn't get to, can I move them to another day?

- Did I plan enough time to get to know my students? How can I plan to get to know them better tomorrow?

- Should I change any seating arrangements that might cause potential behavior problems?

- How did I feel about the day? Was I well prepared? What do I want to do differently tomorrow?

Plan Ahead for a Good First Week

You will concentrate a great deal of energy on the opening day of school, but the first day is only one of many more days to come. Overplan for the first week just as you did for the first day. Review the following activities as you write your lesson plans.

Suggested First Week Activities:

- Introduce classroom jobs. Assign positions.
- Review previously taught skills.
- Administer diagnostic tests.
- Conduct activities that create excitement and anticipation about your content.
- Have students choose free-reading books.
- Continue to get acquainted with each other.
- Play reading and math games.
- Write a positive note to every student in the class.
- Begin sending home positive notes to parents.
- Choose a book and begin reading aloud to the group. Plan a specific time to read each day.

Plan Ways to Create Structure

Your students may feel just as nervous as you do at the beginning of the year. They may wonder what you expect from them at any given point during the day. Creating structure from the start will not only make your job easier, it will help students feel more comfortable and confident. As you plan your first week's agenda and set patterns for the whole year, incorporate the procedures that follow.

Explain the Schedule

Before school begins, develop a daily and a weekly schedule and prepare to adapt it to the needs of your classroom and school. Obviously, your administration will determine class schedules and lunch schedules to some degree. You may also team-teach certain classes with another teacher. Some of your students may attend specialized classes for music, P.E., foreign languages or "pull-out" programs. Individual students may also attend special education classes. Adapt your schedule to these routines and communicate the schedule to students.

Providing structure and consistency will help students learn to organize time. It will also let them know what materials to bring to class so they can begin working immediately. Every plan needs a little flexibility, but use some basic guidelines early in the year and your students will probably perform their work with more focus in later months.

You may want to post a daily schedule on the board. See the following examples.

Sample Schedule for Elementary School

Wednesday in Room 15

8:30	Read silently until bell rings.
8:45	After attendance, meet in reading teams.
9:45	Language Arts writing assignments.
10:30	Recess.
11:00	Math.
11:55	Prepare for lunch.
12:00	Lunch/Recess.
1:00	Review answers to math problems.
1:15	P.E.
2:15	Meet in groups for social studies projects.
2:45	Record homework before going home.

Sample Class Period Schedule for Secondary School

Wednesday in Room 85

9:30	Turn in homework/Groups meet for final preparations.
9:45	Group 1 presentation on the Trail of Tears.
10:00	Group 2 presentation on the Indian Wars.
10:15	Group 3 presentation on Mission Life.
10:30	Record homework assignment before leaving.

Let the Morning Routine Sing

A positive morning activity can help students feel emotionally secure. It can set a tone for friendly interaction with the teacher and other students throughout the day. It can help students focus and it can energize them. You can use a pattern of morning activities to reinforce students' sense of community or you can give students time to collect their thoughts through independent work.

Put some thought into the various ways you can make your morning routine sing. To get started, use the "Activity Ideas: Morning Rituals" on the facing page.

If you teach middle school or high school, look for period-starter ideas instead of morning rituals. During the time you take roll, students need activities that enable them to work quietly and independently, such as listening to music and recording their impressions or beginning the day's written work. For other examples, the morning rituals Poetry Readings and Thoughts for the Day, located on the next page, allow students to work independently as you complete your attendance and other tasks.

Give Clear Assignments

Everyone learns a little differently. Some students respond well to verbal instructions. Others need to read written information. Still other students work best when a teacher offers a hands-on demonstration. Give every student a chance to succeed. Offer all three types of instruction when possible.

You may want to reserve a portion of the chalkboard to list daily or weekly assignments and ask students to check it regularly. Fully explain the assignment and show a sample problem or sample response on the board. The goal is not to keep students guessing at your expectations but to let them invest their energy in doing the work.

Encourage consistency and responsibility by asking students to copy the assignment in their notebooks at the same time each day or period—either as soon as they sit down, right after lunch or at the end of the day. Inform them of a time you will be available if they have questions about the assignment.

When students are absent and cannot copy down the assignments, make it easy for them to know what to do when they return. Set up a corner for make-up assignments by doing the following:

- Label a special basket for each day of the week.
- Place a copy of each day's assignments and worksheets in the basket.
- Tell students that when they miss a day, it is their responsibility to go to the baskets and pick up any work they missed.
- If students fail to pick up the work and complete the assignments within a week after their absence, ask them to write a note to their parents explaining why.

    (You may also want to incorporate the study buddies concept described on page 182 to ensure that students know how to make up missed work.)

Activity Ideas: Morning Rituals

Written Assignments

You may want to begin the day with independent work. If so, write instructions for the first assignment of the day and let students begin their work as soon as they enter the classroom. This encourages self-direction and quiets the classroom before you begin your morning agenda. It also gives you a chance to silently take roll without using valuable learning time.

Class Dialogues

Seat the class in a circle to hold a group meeting in the morning. Ask whether students have any important topics they need to discuss with the class. Then outline the day's schedule, explain what the students can anticipate and generate excitement about the goals for learning. Recap at the end of the day.

You can also use this morning time to formalize a plan for character building. Choose a character trait to discuss each week and talk about ways the students can develop that trait. Let students share their experiences and efforts. Some classes also begin each day reciting an affirmation or a motto about their classroom values or standards. See Chapter 5, "How to Establish a Classroom Community" for ideas.

Sing-alongs

Choose an upbeat song that communicates the attitude you want your students to feel at the beginning of the day. Plan to sing the song for your students on the first day and begin teaching them the lyrics so they can sing it every morning. For younger students, you may want to include hand motions or physical gestures to perform as they sing.

Body Stretches

Exercising the body can help prime the mind. Young students may want to begin the day with a few bending exercises and jumping jacks. The students get their metabolism going before they begin their thinking exercises.

Mind Stretchers

Challenge students to start the day with a riddle that relates to your content. For instance, a student might say, "I'm thinking of a word that means to chuckle loudly. It starts with an L and it is one of this week's spelling words. What is it?" When most or all students have raised their hands, the riddler can choose a student to write the answer on the board.

Poetry Readings

You might want to select a light poetry book geared to your students' grade level and read a poem each morning. Whimsical poems by Shel Silverstein, A.A. Milne and Dr. Seuss will engage younger students and give them something to look forward to each morning, while stimulating their interest in literature. Or you can assign students to bring in poems or books of poems or song lyrics and let the students do the reading.

Thoughts for the Day

Older students can write in their personal journals when they first come to class. They can write about something they hope to accomplish that day or they can respond to a quotation that they select or that you select. You may want to choose quotations by the authors or historical figures your students will study. You'll find many good compilations of quotations in bookstores.

Group Chats

Refer to Chapter 5, "How to Establish a Classroom Community," to explore the benefits of cooperative learning. Have students meet every morning in the same small groups to talk about their studies, their challenges and their plans for the day. Ask each group to come up with a motto and to make a desk card for each member with the motto on it. This little bit of daily bonding helps build peer support for learning throughout the day. The groups change every few months.

Consistently Collect Homework

Students will make homework a habit when they know you have a consistent pattern of assigning and collecting the work. Consider these approaches or come up with a plan of your own. Communicate your plan clearly and stick with it.

- You may want to put a box, bin or "homework hamper" at the front of the room and ask students to deposit the work there as they enter.

- You may set a consistent time each day to have students trade papers and correct one another's work as you read the answers.

- You can assign classroom helpers to collect homework when the bell rings. Rotate homework assistants so everyone has a chance to serve.

Get to Know Your Students

Establishing positive relationships with students boosts their self-esteem and contributes to their success in school. Make an effort to learn as much as you can about your students during the first week of school.

Create a Student Interest Inventory

At the beginning of the year, learn more about your students using one of these information-gathering reproducibles: "Student Interest Inventory" (Elementary), or "Tell Me About You" (Secondary). In addition to learning factual information, you have the opportunity to discover your students' wishes and dreams and their attitudes towards school. This information helps to round out your perceptions of both the outer and inner lives of each student.

Explain to your students that this inventory will help you become better acquainted with each of them. Give them the inventory as the first homework assignment of the year. (Interview younger students in a one-to-one meeting using the inventory as a guide.)

Keep a supply of student interest inventories on hand throughout the year to give to new students entering your classroom.

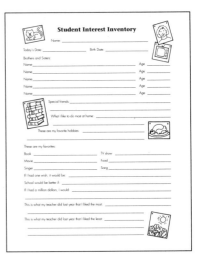

Student Interest Inventory (Elementary)
Page 41

Tell Me About You (Secondary)
Page 42

Get to Know Your Students' Parents

You can also learn a lot about your students by learning about their parents. Send home a brief parent information sheet requesting parents' names, occupations (in case you want to tap their skills or invite them to the class as guest speakers), addresses, and phone numbers. Ask them about their children's past experiences in school and have them describe what they want for their children. This sketch will give you a much better understanding of the student.

For more ideas on how to learn about your students through their parents, read Chapter 3, "How to Involve Parents."

Share Your Own Interests

Create a teacher interest inventory detailing your own likes and dislikes, interests and goals. Distribute a copy of the completed inventory to each student and encourage students to discuss it with you. Getting to know each other will help you build mutually enjoyable and beneficial relationships.

Welcome Classroom Aides

Schools often hire paraprofessionals or classroom aides to support the work of the teachers. Like many other beginning teachers, you may not be sure of the best way to direct the work of an aide. You might also feel a lack of confidence in your authority if the aide has worked at the school for years and comes with a great deal of classroom experience. Put some forethought into how you will make use of classroom aides, and you will probably find it easier to collaborate with confidence during your early teaching career. Take the following steps before school begins.

- Find out what duties your school administration expects the aide to accomplish. Some aides are hired with specially designated funds, and many of their duties have already been determined. (For example, they may work with Title I students to address their specific learning needs.)

- If your aide is assigned to provide general classroom assistance, decide which tasks to assign. You may want help with non-instructional duties such as record keeping or preparing materials. The aide can also assist in instructional activities by working with individual students or with groups of students.

- Plan a meeting with the aide before he or she begins work. Explain your classroom management plan and discuss how the aide can assist you.

- Clearly explain the job you want done. Write down any directions. Give the aide a time frame for each assigned task.

- When the aide begins work, introduce him or her to the class.

- Acknowledge what the aide does well. Offer any suggestions for change in a positive way.

Recruit Volunteers

Your school may not offer you a paid aide. Without an aide, you may want volunteers to help you coordinate your classroom activities, especially if your class includes students of diverse ability levels who each need individual attention. Ask whether your school or parent organization has a list of volunteers or whether you can feel free to recruit volunteers among parents, retired people who live in the neighborhood, or others who want to help children learn.

Volunteers can make your job easier and show students that the whole community supports their learning. Treat your volunteers with appreciation and respect. Carefully plan the ways they will assist you, so they make a meaningful contribution to the class. Take the following steps to prepare for their first visit to the classroom.

- Make your volunteers feel welcome by designating a table or other special location as the volunteer area. Show them where to store personal belongings. Introduce the volunteer to the class, explaining to the students the volunteers' role.

- Prepare for the tasks you assign volunteers by gathering any materials they will need in advance, to prevent disruptions during activities.

- Give clear directions. Write down any directions that might be confusing.

- At the end of the day, warmly thank your volunteers. Send them thank-you notes during the year. Plan an end-of-the-year luncheon or party for the volunteers.

Prepare for a Substitute

Ensure that your students will have good learning experiences even when you are absent. Teachers sometimes leave detailed instructions on what content to cover but forget all the other unknowns that can complicate the school day. How will the teacher know when students need to leave the classroom for a specific program? How will she or he know your plan for classroom discipline? The more the substitute understands your routines, classroom organization and teaching practices, the more consistency he or she will be able to maintain for your students.

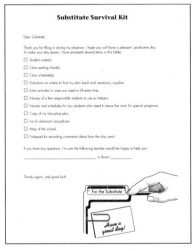

The "Substitute Survival Kit" reproducible, located in the resource section, is a letter you might prepare for a substitute teacher. Collect the listed items early in the school year. Put them in a folder and attach the checklist/letter. Make the folder readily available each time you call a substitute. Find out what phone number you should call when you need a substitute and carry the number with you.

Substitute Survival Kit
Page 43

Put a Discipline Plan in Place

Many new teachers enter the classroom expecting a certain level of automatic respect from students. One teacher reported her shock and dismay when her requests were met with comments such as, "Why should I?" "I don't want to!" and "Make me." Unfortunately, not all students have learned appropriate ways to relate to others, and some are growing up in environments where authority does not necessarily command respect.

New teachers generally find that they experience much better results with students when they set high expectations from the very beginning, make those expectations clear and reinforce their standards with a combination of firmness and positive reinforcement. For these reasons, your first priorities should probably include:

- Developing class rules.
- Teaching them to your students.
- Notifying the parents of your standards for behavior.
- Consistently implementing a discipline plan throughout the year.

One of the secrets of success is to teach specific procedures for activities such as transitioning from one activity to another, working in groups or lining up for recess. Give students plenty of positive reinforcement for following directions correctly.

The following chapter, "How to Manage Behavior," will help you develop, communicate and implement your plan in a positive way. It will also help you learn specific strategies for keeping students on task. If possible, read it and have your plan ready before the school year begins.

Whew! You've made it through your first week. The experience may have raised more questions than answers. Look for the answers in the remainder of this book as you get to know your students and come to understand the secrets of success for teaching them.

Health Emergency Procedures

In case of a student illness or medical emergency, contact:

☐ Main office

☐ Nurse's office

    School nurse's hours: _____

If you do not have a phone in your room, how do you contact the office?

_____

_____

_____

For urgent situations, where can you find first aid supplies?

_____

_____

_____

Who is authorized to administer first aid?

_____

_____

_____

_____

For urgent clean-up needs, contact:

☐ Main office

☐ Custodian

FIRST AID

Lesson Plan Template

Topic: **Grade/Subject:**   **Date(s):**

Learning Objectives:

Materials:

Procedures:

(Can include any combination of elements such as presentation, individual activity, group work, class discussion, review and assessment.)

Homework Assignment (if applicable):

Follow-up Activity:

Supplies Checklist

Supplies for Your Desk

- ☐ Lesson plan book
- ☐ Grade book
- ☐ Attendance book
- ☐ Substitute folder
- ☐ Pencils, pens and markers (including permanent and overhead projector markers)
- ☐ Erasers
- ☐ Scissors
- ☐ Ruler
- ☐ Stapler and staples
- ☐ Staple remover
- ☐ Tape dispenser and extra roll of tape
- ☐ Paper clips
- ☐ Rubber bands
- ☐ Push pins, tacks
- ☐ Glue, paste
- ☐ Hole punch
- ☐ Note paper
- ☐ "Stickies" (Post-it® Notes)
- ☐ Teacher editions of textbooks
- ☐ Dictionary, thesaurus, almanac
- ☐ Oral reading book
- ☐ Clipboard
- ☐ Timer or stopwatch
- ☐ Reward and incentive stickers
- ☐ Rubber stamps and ink pads
- ☐ Index file and cards
- ☐ File folders
- ☐ Small tools (screwdriver, hammer)
- ☐ Box of tissues

Supplies for the Classroom

- ☐ Pencils, crayons, markers
- ☐ Erasers
- ☐ Rulers
- ☐ Glue
- ☐ Writing paper
- ☐ Construction paper (various colors)
- ☐ Math manipulatives
- ☐ Computer disks
- ☐ Scissors
- ☐ Paints and paintbrushes
- ☐ Paint containers (plastic cups, margarine tubs, etc.)
- ☐ Art supplies (yarn, glitter, fabric, etc.)
- ☐ Juice containers
- ☐ 3"-thick pieces of Styrofoam
- ☐ Styrofoam egg cartons
- ☐ Sheets of posterboard
- ☐ Plastic hangers for coats

Other Supplies I Need

- ☐ _____
- ☐ _____
- ☐ _____

Suggested First-Day Activities

Number the activities you plan to include, in the order that you will conduct them.

_____ Make introductions—teacher, students, staff.

_____ Distribute or have students prepare name tags or desk tags.

_____ Take attendance and lunch count.

_____ Give an overview of some of the exciting activities and projects you've planned.

_____ Explain the morning routine pattern.

_____ Tour the classroom. Explain the storage and use of supplies.

_____ Conduct "get acquainted" activities. You may go around the room and have students tell their names and their favorite thing to do.

_____ Assign cubbies, lockers, etc.

_____ Distribute materials (textbooks, pencil, crayons, rulers, etc.).

_____ Read aloud to students (material depends on grade level).

_____ Teach a subject-area lesson with a follow-up art activity. (Keep it simple.)

_____ Sing songs.

_____ Facilitate a creative writing activity.

_____ Ask for a "birthday count" and fill in a birthday chart.

_____ Hand out parent letters and notes from the office.

_____ Assign students to guide new students around the school. If many of your students are attending the school for the first time, include a tour of schoolgrounds for the entire class. (Show restrooms, office, playground, cafeteria.)

_____ Introduce the class rules. (See Chapter 2, "How to Manage Behavior," for more complete suggestions.) Send home a copy of your discipline plan along with a letter of introduction.

_____ Teach specific procedures for different activities as those activities arise.

_____ Take a Student Interest Inventory. (See page 32.)

_____ _____

_____ _____

_____ _____

_____ _____

Mr. Brown Room 6

Welcome Back to School!

Desk Tag

Hello!

My name is

_____

Instructions:

- Fold dotted lines backwards.
- Layer top panel over bottom panel to form a triangle.
- Tape closed.

Student Interest Inventory

Name: _____

Today's Date: _____   Birth Date: _____

Brothers and Sisters:

Name_____   Age _____

Name_____   Age _____

Name_____   Age _____

Name_____   Age _____

Name_____   Age _____

Special friends:_____

_____

What I like to do most at home: _____

_____

These are my favorite hobbies: _____

_____

These are my favorites:

Book _____   TV show _____

Movie _____   Food _____

Singer _____   Song _____

If I had one wish, it would be: _____

School would be better if: _____

If I had a million dollars, I would: _____

_____

This is what my teacher did last year that I liked the most: _____

_____

This is what my teacher did last year that I liked the least: _____

_____

_____

Tell Me About YOU

Welcome to my class! Getting to know you is important to me, and your answers to this survey will help. Your responses will be kept private, so please be honest. If you need more room to answer, use another sheet of paper or the back of this page.

Name: _____ Grade & Class: _____

Teacher: _____ Date: _____

Brothers and Sisters:

Name _____ Age _____

Name _____ Age _____

Name _____ Age _____

Name _____ Age _____

Name _____ Age _____

Special Friends: _____

_____

_____

These are my favorite things to do: _____

_____

These are my favorites:

Book _____ Singer or group _____

Movie _____ Song _____

TV Show _____ Song _____

Some of the things that bug me are: _____

_____

I worry about: _____

_____

School would be better if: _____

_____

This is what a teacher did last year that I really liked: _____

_____

This is what a teacher did last year that bothered or upset me: _____

_____

One goal I'd like to accomplish this year: _____

_____

Substitute Survival Kit

Dear Substitute,

Thank you for filling in during my absence. I hope you will have a pleasant, productive day. To make your day easier, I have enclosed several items in this folder:

☐ Student roster(s).

☐ Class seating chart(s).

☐ Class schedule(s).

☐ Directions on where to find my plan book and necessary supplies.

☐ Extra activities in case you need to fill extra time.

☐ Names of a few responsible students to use as helpers.

☐ Names and schedules for any students who need to leave the room for special programs.

☐ Copy of my discipline plan.

☐ List of classroom procedures.

☐ Map of the school.

☐ Notepad for recording comments about how the day went.

If you have any questions, I'm sure the following teacher would be happy to help you:

_____, in Room _____.

Thanks again, and good luck!

For the Substitute

Have a great day!

CHAPTER 2

How to Manage Behavior

To Tomas,
Thanks for
following directions
in class today!
Mr. Leary

> *" I was worried about spending so much time on classroom rules and procedures and all that stuff. I thought, 'I need to get started on teaching.' But my principal said, 'Don't worry. You have to do this before you can teach.' "*

On the first day of school, you may find that students seem eager to please you. But sooner or later—and usually sooner—you'll notice that some students don't respond to your requests. A few students create disruptions and, suddenly, their attitude seems contagious. You may find yourself asking, "How could I have prevented this? What can I do to regain control of my classroom?"

Don't judge your potential as a teacher based on the behavior of your students, especially during the early weeks of school, but *do* make sure you promptly put your classroom management plan in place. Spend some time before the school year begins thinking through your expectations and designing a plan to help students meet them.

As a new teacher, you will probably want to begin with an approach that creates order and gives students confidence in your leadership. Many beginning teachers use the Assertive Discipline approach because it provides that structure and helps you develop and implement a discipline plan. You will learn some basic Assertive Discipline strategies in this chapter.

Over the course of your career, you will likely want to enhance your approach by adding strategies and exploring other discipline models. You may eventually adopt an eclectic style that reflects your own philosophy and addresses your students' needs. Use the concepts on these pages as the seeds of your ongoing evolution.

Create a Classroom Discipline Plan

During the first days and weeks of school, the most important lesson you teach may be how to behave at school. The time you spend teaching classroom rules early in the year could save you discipline time throughout the year. In fact, effective elementary teachers often spend more than a third of their first week in school teaching rules and procedures, and middle school teachers may spend one fourth of their time teaching them.

Remember, practice makes perfect. So to help students learn appropriate behavior, you can't just tell them the rules. You must provide opportunities for practice.

The discipline plan outlined in this section is based on the Assertive Discipline approach. Please note that this overview simplifies a complex topic. You can find further guidelines for developing your discipline plan by reading other books on classroom management. Meanwhile, begin to develop your classroom discipline plan based on a few basic elements.

Elements of an Effective Classroom Discipline Plan

1. **Rules:** A few simple rules that students observe at all times.

2. **Consequences:** To stop the misbehavior and help students reflect on how to better follow the rules.

3. **Positive recognition:** To help students follow the rules consistently so you can be free to teach.

Establish Class Rules for Behavior

Think carefully about the behaviors you really need to require of your students in order to maintain a positive, safe environment, then choose a maximum of five rules. Rules are standards that remain in place at all times, while procedures vary according to the activity. Follow these guidelines in establishing the class rules.

- Make sure rules are observable. Avoid vague rules such as "be good" in favor of more specific rules.

- Include the key rule, "Follow directions." This rule enables you to introduce more specific procedures throughout the day and throughout the year.

- State the rules in a positive way whenever possible. Children often act in response to the actual images your words suggest, so help them visualize the positive rather than the negative behavior. Instead of saying, "Don't push in line," say "Keep your hands, feet and objects to yourself."

- Discuss the rules with your students. Explain the rationale for each rule, or guide students, through class discussion, to draw their own conclusions about the importance of the rule.

- Record the rules on a chart and post it where students will see it often. The samples below indicate the types of rules appropriate for various grade levels.

Sample Elementary School Rules

- Follow directions.
- Keep hands, feet and objects to yourself.
- Ask for permission to leave the room.
- Use appropriate language.
- Use a low-level voice in the classroom.

Sample Secondary School Rules

- Follow directions.
- Be in your seat when the bell rings.
- Bring all necessary materials to class.

Choose Appropriate Consequences

When students stray off task without disrupting the class, use the redirecting techniques listed on pages 58 and 59 to encourage them to correct their own behavior. Yet despite your best efforts, students will occasionally act out, disregard the rules and disturb the class. At this point, you will need to enforce consequences to stop the disruptive behavior. Planning these consequences in advance can ensure that you react consistently and fairly to disruptions.

Consequences need not be severe to produce results. The inevitability, not the severity, of a consequence makes it effective. Minimal consequences, often the easiest to implement, can motivate change without humiliating the student or interfering with the learning.

Your basic discipline plan should contain a maximum of five consequences. List these consequences in a progressive hierarchy, starting with a warning, then adding gradually more severe consequences each time the student chooses to disrupt within a school day.

The first time the student breaks a rule, for instance, you might simply give a reminder. The second time may warrant two minutes of reflection time away from the group. The third time the student breaks the rule in the same day, you might set up a private conference with the student. When using such a hierarchy, do not carry over the consequences into the next day. Students should start each day with a clean slate. However, your hierarchy should include a "severe clause" to use when a student becomes defiant or violent. In such a case, you may skip all the other steps and send the student directly to the principal's office.

In addition to those consequences listed above, consider the following possibilities:

- Written assignment in behavior journal.

- Loss of a special privilege.

- Staying after school for a few minutes.

- Last to leave the class.

Whenever possible, incorporate logical consequences and opportunities for reflection. For instance, if you sent a student to "time-out" for tearing pages from a classmate's book, also require that the student repair the book. Time-out provides a good opportunity for a student to fill out a "Think Sheet" to make productive use of the isolation period. (If you do choose to use "time out" as a consequence, make sure you know your school's policies regarding isolating students from the group.) A "Think Sheet" reproducible is provided in the resource section at the end of this chapter. At the end of the period, when the student has calmed down and completed the "Think Sheet," conduct a private conversation about the behavior. Discuss what better choices the student might make next time.

Think Sheet
Page 64

See page 59 for suggestions on how to implement your plan.

Plan for Positive Reinforcement

Positive support can reduce the need for discipline. Your overall behavior management plan should help students feel motivated to make responsible choices on their own, but some students may not immediately feel compelled to follow rules or make wise choices. They may, in the beginning, need reinforcement from the outside. Your encouragement can help them practice good behavior until it becomes a habit or a natural choice. So your classroom discipline plan should emphasize positive reinforcement rather than just negative consequences for misbehavior.

Recognition for a job well done is appreciated by students of any age. Even secondary students, no matter how "cool" they appear to be, are no different from any of us when we are presented with tangible evidence that someone has noticed our good work. They may stuff the "award" in a book with scarcely a glance, but chances are good that that piece of paper will be taken out later at home, read carefully and perhaps even tucked away among the student's mementos.

Praise as Positive Reinforcement

You might be surprised to discover the power of praise to motivate behavior. When you take the time to say something positive to a student, you convey the message, "I care about you, I notice your good efforts, and I'm proud of you."

Older students often do not want to be singled out publicly for praise, but you can still acknowledge appropriate behavior with handwritten notes, a nod, a pat on the back, or a word with the student after class.

When you deliver praise, always make it genuine. Insincere praise weakens its effectiveness as a behavior incentive and does little to boost a student's self-esteem. Early adolescents, especially, know whether or not their behavior is appropriate. They may resent actions they consider "phony" on the part of adults, so make your praise constructive and meaningful, and keep the following pointers in mind:

- Use specific, descriptive praise. If you simply say, "Good job," you have missed a chance to reinforce an action that shows student growth and improvement. Effective praise takes note of the specific improvement you have observed and lets the student know how he, she—or the entire class—benefits from that improvement. Example: "You did a great job collecting the math materials and putting them away in the correct folder. You realized that the students will be able to find those materials easily tomorrow. That really helps the class."

- Personalize your praise. Mention the student's name. Remember to use eye contact. It assures the student of your sincerity.

- Encourage students to praise one another.

- When you give an instruction, comment on those who are following the directions correctly rather than pointing out those who are proceeding incorrectly.

- Acknowledge student participation by thanking students for their answers, thoughts and ideas.

- Recognize and acknowledge students with positive notes and phone calls home.

- Reinforce small deeds or positive behaviors with praise.

Look for opportunities to praise students by posting the "50 Opportunities to Say 'You're Terrific'" reproducible provided in the resource section. Then create your own plan of action for positive reinforcement using the "PR (Positive Reminder) Plan" reproducible.

50 Opportunities to Say "You're Terrific"
Page 65

P.R. (Positive Reminder) Plan
Page 66

Positive Notes

In addition to giving praise, reinforce positive student behavior with notes given to students and sent home to parents. Reproduce a stack of the "Positive Notes" in the resource section to keep on your desktop, and distribute them frequently to all students. Often it is only the "superstars" who receive recognition, and you don't want to overlook students who make minor improvements in their behavior, or the students who may be quiet or withdrawn. Try to make sure that all students receive an equal number of notes as the year progresses.

Classwide Recognition

Group goals can influence behavior. Occasional group rewards can help students behave responsibly while creating a sense of "family" in your classroom. In the beginning of the year, as you strive to help students learn procedures and develop positive group habits, you may want to offer a classwide incentive. Later in the year, when you notice the need for the entire class to work on changing a habit or behavior, a classwide reward system can, again, help set a higher standard. For example, if students come in late from recess every day, you might offer a classwide reward for promptness. In anticipation of the reward, students will remind one another to line up on time.

Positive Notes (Elementary)
Page 67–68

Positive Notes (Secondary)
Page 69–70

Activity Idea:
Positives for the Entire Class

Set up the contingency that when the entire class earns a predetermined number of points for meeting your expectations for behavior, they will receive a special reward. Whenever the whole class exhibits that behavior (for example, by quietly entering the classroom after recess), the whole class earns a point. Keep track of the points on the chalkboard or with stickers on a bulletin board. Once you award a point, do not take it away for misconduct.

You may want to reward the class with one or more of the following options.

- Free time in class
- Time in class to do homework
- Popcorn while watching a video
- Special arts and crafts projects
- Play radio or CDs in class
- Movie or cartoons
- Extra P.E. time

- Special lunch or dessert
- Field trip
- Conduct class on the lawn
- Cook in class
- Public recognition of group by principal
- Special class visitor (firefighter, magician)

List the Elements of Your Plan

Now that you have considered the three elements of your classroom discipline plan, draft your own personal plan. Use the "Classroom Discipline Plan" worksheet provided in the resource section to identify the rules, consequences and positive reinforcement you will use. Refer to the examples that follow on this and the next two pages for ideas. Remember to limit your rules to three—or at most, five—and make sure you emphasize the desired behavior rather than the undesirable behavior. Add specific methods of positive recognition, then arrange your consequences in a hierarchy.

Classroom Discipline Plan
Page 71

Sample Classroom Discipline Plan
Elementary

Classroom Rules

Follow directions.

Keep hands, feet and objects to yourself.

No teasing or name calling.

Positive Recognition

Praise

First in line for recess

Positive notes sent home to parents

Positive notes to students

Eat lunch with teacher

Select own seat on Friday

Consequences

First time student breaks a rule: . . . . Warning

Second time: . . . . 5 minutes working away from group

Third time: . . . . 10 minutes working away from group

Fourth time: . . . . Teacher calls parents

Fifth time: . . . . Send to principal

Severe clause: . . . . Send to principal

Sample Classroom Discipline Plan
Middle

Classroom Rules

Follow directions.

Keep hands, feet and objects to yourself.

No swearing, teasing or name calling.

Positive Recognition

Praise

Positive notes sent home to parents

Positive notes to students

Coupons for student store

Select own seat for the day

No-homework pass

Consequences

First time student breaks a rule: . . . . Warning

Second time: . . . . Stay in class 1 minute after the bell

Third time: . . . . Stay in class 2 minutes after the bell

Fourth time: . . . . Teacher calls parents

Fifth time: . . . . Send to principal

Severe clause: . . . . Send to principal

Sample Classroom Discipline Plan
Secondary

Classroom Rules

Follow directions.

Take your seat before the bell rings.

Bring required materials to class.

Positive Recognition	Additional positives may include:
Praise	Coupons for student store
Positive notes sent home to parents	Select own seat for the day
Positive notes to students	No-homework pass
Positive phone calls to students and parents	Coupons and raffle tickets

Consequences

First time student breaks a rule: . . . . Warning

Second time: . . . . Stay in class 1 minute after the bell

Third time: . . . . 5 minutes detention during lunch or after school

Fourth time: . . . . Teacher calls parents

Fifth time: . . . . Send to principal

Severe clause: . . . . Send to principal

Plan for Spring Fever

Remember that toward the end of the school year, as students become restless and ready for vacation, the need for structure may become even more apparent in your classroom. Plan to incorporate individual and classwide positive recognition to remind students to stay on track.

Consider the Long-Term Effects of Discipline

You will find that while maintaining order seems especially important in the beginning, you also need to consider the long-term benefits of a plan that emphasizes discipline, not punishment. As you design your discipline plan, consider the points Luann Fulbright made in the June 1998 issue of the journal "Better Teaching" regarding the intent of a consequence.

Is It Discipline or Punishment?

What's the difference between discipline and punishment? Punishment is coercive; discipline is educational.

If you are striving to create a climate that encourages discipline, here are some things to think about:

Punishment:

- **Is concerned with what happened** (the past).
- **Is based on the power** of an authority.
- **Closes options** for the individual, who must pay for a behavior that has already occurred.
- **Is easy and expedient.**
- **Focuses on strategies intended to control** the behavior of the learner.
- **Rarely results in positive changes** in behavior; at best, produces compliance. At worst, punishment produces resentment and provokes a desire for revenge.

Discipline:

- **Is concerned with what is happening now** (present).
- **Is based on rules that students must learn** and accept to function in society.
- **Opens options** for the individual, who can choose new behavior.
- **Can be difficult** and time consuming.
- **Focuses on the learner's behavior** and the consequences of that behavior.
- **Usually results in a change** in behavior that is more successful, acceptable and responsible than that produced by punishment.

Source: Richard Bodine, Donna Crawford & Fred Schrumpf, *Creating the Peaceable School Program Guide*, Research Press, 2612 N. Mattis Ave., Champaign, IL 61821.

Present Your Plan

When students know your expectations for behavior, they can work to achieve them. When parents and administrators know your plan of action, they can support it. Share the details of your discipline plan so you can act quickly and decisively for more effective results.

Launch your plan by taking the following steps.

Share Your Plan with Your Administrator

You will feel more confident about presenting your discipline plan if you know you have the support of your administrator. Prepare a copy of your classroom discipline plan for your administrator's approval. Make sure that you both understand the role he or she will play in your plan. Discuss your expectations of what will take place when you send a student to the principal. Ask for the administrator's input and listen to any suggested changes. Also, discuss what will happen if the principal is not in the building.

Present Your Plan to Parents

On the first day of school, send home a letter to introduce yourself to parents. You will find suggestions for doing so on page 79 in Chapter 3. Include a second letter that outlines your discipline plan and provides a detachable sign-off portion for parents to verify that they have read and understand your plan.

Teach Your Plan to Students

Students need a clear understanding of your expectations and of what they can expect from you in return. Teach your discipline plan just as you would teach any other subject or skill. Write your rules, positives and consequences on a large poster to use as a visual aid as you proceed through the lesson. (Display the poster permanently in a prominent location in your classroom to serve as a reminder to students. See the sample plans on page 52–53.) Use a positive tone as you explain the components of your plan.

Agenda for Teaching Your Plan

1. **Rules:** Explain why the class needs rules. (Rules help create a safe environment where each student can learn.) Explain the rules and discuss and demonstrate them, especially with younger students.

2. **Positive recognition:** Explain how you will recognize students for following rules and directions.

3. **Consequences:** Explain why the discipline plan includes consequences and emphasize that you will only apply them as a result of students' own behavior choices. Explain the consequences and how you will implement them.

4. **Check for understanding:** Have students explain the plan and demonstrate the rules. Explain that in addition to these basic rules, students will learn procedures to follow each time they participate in a new type of activity.

Teach Procedures

Your classroom discipline plan lists the general rules you expect students to follow at all times. In addition to teaching general classroom rules, you will need to teach more specific procedures to keep the classroom running smoothly during a particular type of activity.

Use the "Procedures I Will Teach Early in the Year" checklist in the resource section to decide which procedures you need to teach your students in the first few days and weeks of school. Check off the situations that would flow more smoothly if students learned specific procedures. For instance, you may be surprised at how quickly your classroom can become noisy, especially when students move around the room. This can happen on many occasions: when students move into small groups for activities, when they go to work at learning centers, or when they pass out materials to each other.

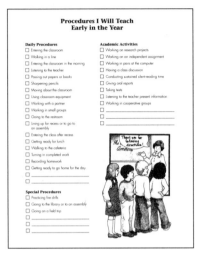

Procedures I Will Teach Early in the Year
Page 72

The first time you conduct a new activity—for instance, one that requires students to move about the classroom or to leave the classroom—plan a lesson to teach students the procedures for the transition. The example on the next page, "Sample Procedure for Transitioning from the Classroom," shows how you can make your instructions explicit and gear them to the age and understanding of your students.

When you teach procedures or give directions, keep these suggestions in mind.

- Give simple information first, let students ask questions, then give more details. Students won't hear the specifics if they're still grappling with the main objectives.

- Rehearse the instructions before you present them to the class. Listen to yourself to check for clarity. Imagine students trying to follow the instructions as you explain them.

- Reinforce the instructions. Write them on the board, put them on a transparency, distribute a handout or draw a diagram. Some students need visual cues rather than just hearing the instructions.

- Have students role-play the transition or practice the procedure you want them to learn so their response will become automatic each time you give the direction in the future.

- For younger students, assign "buddies" to help each other when following new procedures. This will eliminate the need for you to try to assist all your students at once. (See page 182 for more ideas on how to use buddies.)

Sample Procedure
for Transitioning from the Classroom

1. **Outline the procedure on the chalkboard.**
   - Line up single file.
   - Keep your hands by your sides.
   - Walk without talking.
   - Do not run.

2. **Have volunteer students read the directions aloud.**

3. **Explain your rationale.**

   Tell students why it is important for them to follow these directions. Discuss with your students the reasons for walking quietly:

   - Safety is the most important reason for observing good walking procedures. Students who run might trip and hurt themselves or someone else.
   - Walking in line is a manageable way to get from one place to another. The class stays together.
   - Classes that move quietly through the halls show respect for other classes by not disrupting their learning.
   - The class's behavior in line reflects their ability to follow directions and to function as a group.

4. **Question students for understanding.**

5. **Ask what walking quietly looks like and sounds like.**

   Have the class role-play following these directions, or else have one student play the role of the teacher and give the direction to the students.

6. **Following the lesson, *immediately* begin the activity to which the procedure applies.**

   For instance, plan this activity right before a trip to another point outside the classroom.

   - Make sure that students walk quietly and keep their hands to themselves. Have students practice the correct behaviors.
   - Monitor students as they walk in line. Avoid walking at the front with your back toward students; walk in the middle, turning often, or at the end. Praise and reward students for following the correct procedures.

7. **Review these directions prior to taking another trip outside the room.**

Redirect Off-Task Behavior

Your behavior management plan expresses the boundaries for student behavior in the same way that the white markers on a football field tell a player he or she is out-of-bounds. Yet within those boundaries, the players can conduct a wide range of activities. In the same way, you can influence student behavior with many strategies that curtail a problem before you have to impose consequences. When students stray from the task at hand, you can refocus their attention with these simple techniques.

The Freeze

Noise and confusion in the classroom sometimes lead to more of the same. Some new teachers do not know what to do when the situation escalates out of control. Teach students to "freeze" when signaled by a physical gesture such as raising your hand, flipping the light switch, clapping or creating a noise with a bell. When students hear or see the signal, they should then refocus their attention on you so you can give them a specific direction on what to do next.

When using the freeze to stop one student who has strayed off task, state what you want the student to do in a clear, positive way rather than making an ultimatum. For instance, say, "Bob, please return to your seat," instead of "Bob, return to your seat now or I'll give you five minutes of detention."

The Look

You may remember from your own childhood a mother's or father's expression that communicated disapproval of your behavior. Use this redirecting technique in your own classroom. When a student doodles during a discussion or students in a cooperative group joke around instead of sticking to the activity, establish eye contact with the student or group. Maintain a firm, calm look and students will generally correct their own behavior before you have to say a single word.

Proximity

Effective teachers move purposefully around the classroom and use their physical presence to redirect students who are off task. For example, you may notice that a student is staring out the window instead of listening to another student's presentation. Stand next to him or her without calling attention verbally to the behavior. Remain there until the student rejoins the group.

Changing Seating Arrangements

You still may notice, over time, that students exhibit more off-task behavior in certain parts of the room than in others. (For instance, a student in the back row may not hear or see well and may become more easily distracted.) You can curtail or prevent behavioral problems by periodically changing your seating arrangement. Separate students who tend to chat, or move a student who is frequently off task to a location near the front of the room.

By relocating all the students from time to time, you may change the classroom dynamics enough to eliminate the problem. However, remember to balance the benefits of stability with the benefits of change. Choose a seating arrangement that will encourage improvements in behavior and learning and will still provide a convenient format for group activities. You will find several sample seating arrangements on page 21 in Chapter 1 and more ideas on page 175 in Chapter 5.

Mentioning a Student's Name

A student who is not paying attention will perk up at the sound of his or her name. Try weaving the student's name into the lesson material. For instance, you could start a math problem with, "Eddy and Derrick went fishing. They each caught 14 fish. How many did they catch together?" Eddy and Derrick will probably sit up and listen as you continue speaking and yet will not feel that you singled them out in front of the class.

2

Implement Your Plan

Review the information throughout this chapter and use the following guidelines to minimize the level and frequency of discipline needed in your classroom as you implement the plan.

- Make sure you have prepared lessons and activities that will engage your students.

- Make certain students understand the rules and consequences.

- Fully explain procedures for tasks and activities and check students' understanding.

- Remember to recognize positive behavior after giving students directions or assigning work.

- When students stray off task, use redirecting techniques. (See page 58.)

- If you must administer consequences for disruptions, walk up to the student and speak calmly, quietly and firmly.

- As soon as the student corrects the behavior, recognize the positive action.

- When disruptive behavior persists, hold reflective conversations with the student and conferences with parents and administrators to help the student make a change. See the next two pages for suggestions.

- Document all warnings and consequences given throughout the day.

- Keep your standards high and your expectations for behavior consistent. Students may become restless during a change in routine such as a field trip or assembly, or at the end of the year. They may need more structure than usual at these times.

Reach Out to Difficult Students

If you adhere to a consistent discipline plan, most of your students will follow your rules and expectations. You may have one or two students, however, who require special attention because of disruptive or belligerent behavior.

One reason some students do not meet behavioral expectations at school may be because they have experienced failure in the past. By reaching out to these students, you can begin to restore high self-expectations and the tendency to take responsibility for their own behavior. You can help them see that at least one caring adult wants to help them succeed.

Follow these guidelines for building a constructive relationship with a difficult student.

- Imagine how you would feel and how you would perceive school if you were that student. Realize that students who often feel rejection, abandonment or disapproval are likely to develop a negative reflex or to respond to a given situation with a disproportionate level of anger.

- Take a proactive position in your effort to restore the student's trust level. Build a bridge by taking the time to talk personally with the student. Convey that you have high expectations for the student's success.

- If the student rebuffs you, avoid acting hurt, angry or defensive. Just continue to help the student see the relationship between effort and outcome, and help the student discover a special talent or develop a new skill that will help him or her experience the intrinsic joy of learning.

Consider this scenario: A student's negative expectations interfere with his ability to trust and get along with his classmates and teachers. The teacher begins spending time with him after school, teaching him math skills that challenge him cognitively and restore his sense of self-esteem.

The teacher asks the student to demonstrate the new skills to the class, so the student becomes a unique contributor to the other students' learning. As the student's trust of his teacher and peers increases, the whole classroom community enjoys the benefits.

Conduct One-on-One Conferences

Your sense of fulfillment as a new teacher may depend on your ability to maintain a positive learning environment for the whole class while expressing sensitivity with individual students. These expressions generally happen in private conversations. Many teachers find that the listening skills they exercise can help students work through problems that affect not only their learning and their behavior but their sense of well-being.

When you suspect that a student's difficult behavior may result from an emotional trauma or a negative self-image, hold a private conversation with the student, keeping in mind that as you exercise empathy, you also need to help the student strive for a desired outcome. Initiate a private conference and conduct the following steps:

1. Express your concerns.
2. Get the student's point of view.
3. Offer to help. Let the student know you care but also clarify your expectations.
4. Ask what the student can do to help solve the problem.
5. Discuss the choices available to the student.
6. Agree on a solution that supports your standards for learning and behavior while meeting the student's needs.
7. If necessary, teach the applicable skills, such as anger management, to the student. (See Chapter 6, "How to Teach Social Skills.")
8. Set up a follow-up meeting and monitor the student's progress.
9. If necessary, plan a conference with the parents, the school counselor or a team of faculty members to address the student's problems.

If the student has serious needs or problems, this process may open the door to getting the extra help needed. It will also show the student that you care and can help. Your consciousness raising and encouragement may be just what the student needs to get back on track.

When meeting with adolescents, keep in mind that they do not want to be *told* what to do. They want to feel they have a say in how they choose to behave. Whenever possible, involve the student in discussing how he or she could change behavior. Listen carefully to the student's input and give credence to his or her thoughts.

Plan your meeting with the student using the reproducible "Teacher-Student Problem-Solving Conference Worksheet" provided in the resource section.

Teacher-Student
Problem-Solving Conference
Worksheet
Page 73

Change One Behavior at a Time

The goal of your conference is to stop the misbehavior not only in the short run but in the long run. However, the student may feel overwhelmed about the needed changes you identify together in a conference, and you too may not be sure where to begin. Use this rule of thumb: Rather than working on all aspects of a student's behavior, focus on one behavior at a time. Set an achievable goal together.

If the student continually talks to friends while the teacher offers instruction, you might encourage him or her to set the goal, "I will listen quietly while the teacher gives directions," rather than "I will always be quiet." Keep your expectations realistic. Monitor the student's progress and help the student keep the promise.

Conduct Group Conferences

If you have tried to change this one behavior through one-on-one problem solving as well as through your classroom discipline plan and the problem persists, you may need to involve the parents and principal and draw up an individualized behavior contract. Use the "Behavior Contract" reproducible in the resource section. Again, keep the goal of the contract specific and you will find it easier to measure the student's improvement.

To use the contract, take the following steps:

1. Explain the problem to the principal and ask for support.

2. Schedule a meeting with the principal, the parent and the student.

3. Rather than telling the student what he or she did, ask the student to describe the behavior and its impact on others.

4. Ask the student to explain what he or she will do differently in the future.

5. Through joint discussion, agree on positive and negative consequences.

6. Have the student, parent, principal and teacher each sign the agreement.

7. Schedule a follow-up meeting to assess whether the student honored the contract.

Keeping the behavior contract on file will help you remain proactive if a student persists in disruptive behavior. It will help you individualize and document your plan of action.

Behavior Contract
Page 74

Document All Behavior Problems

A beginning teacher may not realize the importance of recording behavior problems until, days after an incident occurs, an administrator or a parent asks for an account of what happened. Suddenly, the teacher feels unsure of the facts.

To avoid such a situation, use the "Behavior Documentation Sheet" reproducible in the resource section to keep accurate, factual records of how your students behave both in the classroom and in other situations (in line, at assemblies, etc.). The more documentation you can show, the easier it will be to get the assistance you need from administrators and parents. You will, ideally, have recorded several of these behavior problems on the sheet before approaching the principal, parents and student to develop a behavior contract.

Behavior Documentation Sheet
Page 75

Documentation Idea:
Keep a File on Each Student

Teachers have used index cards, notes in the plan book and other ideas for documenting behavior problems. One of the best ways to keep track of incidents is to keep a file folder for every student. The folder can include notes from conferences, letters from parents, and report cards. It can also include the parent information sheets referred to under "Get to Know Your Students' Parents" on page 33 and any think sheets, behavior contracts or conference-planning worksheets. This way, if you need to call a parent in the evening, you can pull out the file, take it home and have all the information at your fingertips rather than having to look it up by date.

When an incident occurs, record the following information and insert it in the folder or write directly on the folder.

- Date and time of incident

- Factual, specific description of incident

- Actions taken

- Parent contact made (type and date)

- Input from parent and actions you and parent agree upon

- Follow-up actions and any further contact with parents

Example

Incident:

> Nov. 18
> Frank had three bullying incidents in one day:
> — shoved Preston in hallway
> — hid Preston's notebook after recess
> — tripped him by the pencil sharpener

Actions taken:

> Private conference with Frank.
> Also changed his seat.

Parent contact made:

> Nov. 19
> Phoned Frank's father. We agreed Frank would spend time helping me in the classroom after school every time he bullies someone.
> Will call Frank's dad with weekly updates.

Follow-up:

> November 25
> Called Frank's parents — good report.

Think Sheet

What I did:

_____

_____

_____

What effect my actions had on others:

_____

_____

_____

What I could have done:

_____

_____

_____

What effect this action would have on others:

_____

_____

_____

What I will do differently next time:

_____

_____

_____

50 Opportunities to Say "You're Terrific"

There are hundreds of opportunities to praise students each day of the year. Don't let these moments slip by.

Praise students for:

1. Entering the classroom quietly.
2. Putting away coat and backpack.
3. Cooperating while teacher takes attendance.
4. Returning permission slips and school forms on time.
5. Transitioning into an activity appropriately.
6. Following directions.
7. Saying "please" and "thank you."
8. Listening attentively.
9. Helping a classmate.
10. Lining up appropriately.
11. Turning in homework.
12. Being a good audience at an assembly.
13. Beginning work right away.
14. Asking questions when unsure.

15. Good behavior during a test.
16. Participating in a class discussion.
17. Walking appropriately in the halls.
18. Working cooperatively with a partner.
19. Good behavior during a field trip.
20. Cleaning up.
21. Extra effort on an assignment.
22. Assisting a new student.
23. Remembering to shuttle correspondence or permission slips to and from parents.
24. Making up missed assignments.
26. Extra effort on a long-term project.
27. Sharing.
28. Being sensitive to others' feelings.
29. Learning a new skill.
30. Appropriate use of school property.
31. Returning borrowed books and materials.

32. Showing enthusiasm.
33. Being responsible for a classroom job.
34. Offering help without being asked.
35. Not wasting paper and supplies.
37. Telling the truth.
38. Accepting a new challenge.
39. Behaving when a guest is in the room.
40. Reading at home.
41. Participating in school functions.
42. Demonstrating a positive attitude.
43. Giving one's best effort.
44. Returning from the yard quietly.
45. Participating in a group activity.
46. Using problem-solving skills.
47. Showing creativity.
48. Keeping busy when work is finished.
49. Taking turns.
50. Working cooperatively within a group.

P.R. (Positive Reminder) Plan

Preview the strategies below and incorporate them into your lesson plans. Gradually add and vary your techniques for reinforcement. When you feel ready, assess yourself to see how many times you implement one or more of the following strategies within the course of a week.

1. **"Catch students being good."** Write it in your plan book or on a sticky note on your desk so you will watch for and reinforce positive behavior. (See the reproducible, "50 Opportunities to Say 'You're Terrific!'")

2. **Fairly distribute your praise.** Each time you acknowledge a student for positive behavior during class, jot down his or her name or initials. Keep track of whom you praise and how often.

3. **Set a "praise goal" for each class.** For example, try to praise several students per period so that within a week you will have acknowledged every student you teach. This exercise can prove especially helpful in developing the habit of seeing the good in every student.

4. **Set a weekly goal for positive notes home.** Remember the importance of positive notes or phone calls home in motivating students and creating rapport with parents. Set a goal of several calls or notes a week to ensure that you contact each student's family during the semester.

Praise Goals and Plans for the Week

_____

_____

_____

_____

_____

_____

_____

_____

_____

_____

_____

_____

_____

_____

_____

A Message for You

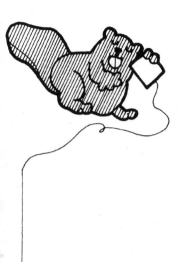

Wanted You to Know

Dear _____ ,

_____ had a

great day today because

_____

_____

_____

Signed

_____

Date

Certificate of Merit

Official
Blue Ribbon
Award

presented to _____

for _____

_____

_____

Student's Signature

_____

Teacher's Signature

_____

Date

A note from the teacher

_____
Subject   Period

A note from the teacher

_____
Subject   Period

A note from the teacher

$+$ $\div$ $=$ $\%$

_____
Subject   Period

A note from the teacher

_____
Subject   Period

Classroom Discipline Plan

Rules

_____

_____

_____

_____

_____

Positives

_____

_____

_____

_____

_____

_____

_____

_____

_____

Consequences

_____

_____

_____

_____

_____

Procedures I Will Teach
Early in the Year

Daily Procedures

- [ ] Entering the classroom
- [ ] Walking in a line
- [ ] Entering the classroom in the morning
- [ ] Listening to the teacher
- [ ] Passing out papers or books
- [ ] Sharpening pencils
- [ ] Moving about the classroom
- [ ] Using classroom equipment
- [ ] Working with a partner
- [ ] Working in small groups
- [ ] Going to the restroom
- [ ] Lining up for recess or to go to an assembly
- [ ] Entering the class after recess
- [ ] Getting ready for lunch
- [ ] Walking to the cafeteria
- [ ] Turning in completed work
- [ ] Recording homework
- [ ] Getting ready to go home for the day
- [ ] _____
- [ ] _____

Special Procedures

- [ ] Practicing fire drills
- [ ] Going to the library or to an assembly
- [ ] Going on a field trip
- [ ] _____
- [ ] _____
- [ ] _____

Academic Activities

- [ ] Working on research projects
- [ ] Working on an independent assignment
- [ ] Working in pairs at the computer
- [ ] Having a class discussion
- [ ] Conducting sustained silent-reading time
- [ ] Giving oral reports
- [ ] Taking tests
- [ ] Listening to the teacher present information
- [ ] Working in cooperative groups
- [ ] _____
- [ ] _____
- [ ] _____

Teacher-Student Problem-Solving Conference Worksheet

Student's Name: _____

Class/Grade: _____ Date: _____

Problem (and reasons for your concern):

_____

_____

Student input as to why problem is occurring:

_____

_____

Steps you can take to help:

_____

_____

Actions student can take to solve problem:

_____

_____

Summarize conference (restate your behavior expectations):

_____

_____

Follow-up/Comments:

_____

_____

_____

_____

Behavior Contract

Date: _____   Student's Name: _____

This student has agreed to try to improve his or her behavior and promises to:

_____

_____

_____

If the student does as agreed, the student will:

_____

_____

If the student does not fulfill the agreement, the student will:

_____

_____

This contract will be in effect for: _____

_____   _____
Student's Signature   Teacher's Signature

_____   _____
Parent's Signature   Principal's Signature

Behavior Documentation Sheet

Student: _____   Teacher: _____

Grade/Period: _____   Parent(s): _____

Home Phone: _____   Work Phone: _____

Date and Time	Problem Behavior What did you observe? List facts: specific behaviors, where it happened, who was involved.	Actions Taken Describe your responses to the misbehavior including actions for positively encouraging improvement and parent contact.

Results of Actions Taken _____

Results of Actions Taken _____

Results of Actions Taken _____

Results of Actions Taken _____

Results of Actions Taken _____

CHAPTER 3

How to Involve Parents

" I was so hesitant to make that first phone call to a parent. But it was great. She thanked me for calling. We had a conference, and it changed everything. I thought, 'Gosh, I should have called a long time ago.' "

Parents can do a lot to influence students' attitudes toward learning, yet many teachers do not fully tap this potential resource. Some teachers have not received much training in working with parents or may feel hesitant to ask for parents' support. At the same time, not all parents have had good experiences with schools or teachers and may not trust institutions. In these cases, it becomes especially important that the teacher reach out, build a trusting relationship and encourage a parent's involvement.

Once you realize what an asset parents represent, you will want to allay their concerns and engage them as partners in the learning process. Parents can give you valuable information about their children's learning needs. They can also support your homework goals and facilitate enrichment activities at home. They can help their children learn relevant skills as well as study habits and approaches to problem solving. The confidence parents convey in you will build support that you may need later in the year if the student faces difficulties.

Take the time to earn the parents' confidence and trust, because when you cultivate a sense of partnership with parents, you magnify your own potential to influence your students. In this chapter, you will learn how to proactively involve parents and how to address problems that may arise. You'll find plenty of resources and reproducibles to help you keep the communication flowing.

Communicate Through Correspondence

There's something special about a piece of "mail" that a student carries home to a parent. For one thing, it lets the student know that the teacher and parents are communicating. Research shows that student performance improves when students see parents and teachers interacting in a positive way about student learning. And a parent's positive feelings about school can nurture the sense of security and well-being the student needs to thrive. So when you send positive communications home that foster good will between students and parents, you strengthen your classroom environment. This section outlines several means of correspondence that can cement the three-way bond between student, teacher and parent.

Say Hello in a Letter

A letter of introduction at the beginning of the year will let parents know that you want to include them as partners in your students' learning. Keep the length under a page. Make the tone upbeat and enthusiastic. Take this opportunity to tell parents that you need their support and that you consider the education of their children a team effort. Include in your letter:

- Information about your professional background.
- Your personal interests (hobbies, travels, etc.).
- Your educational plans and special activities for the upcoming school year.
- A statement expressing your confidence in the success you expect for all your students.

See the example "Looking Forward to a Great New Year" on the next page to plan your introductory letter. Plan to send home a copy of your homework policy, perhaps as your next piece of correspondence. (See page 87.) Then follow up with weekly contact with your students' parents. You'll find several ideas for positive, caring correspondence in this section. Also look for information on page 33 ("Get to Know Your Students' Parents").

Looking Forward to a Great New Year

Dear Parent:

My name is Mr. Robert Marquez, and I will be your child's sixth-grade teacher this year. I will spend a great deal of time with your child in the upcoming school year. Because of this, I'd like to take this opportunity to tell you a few things about myself—both personally and professionally.

I was born and raised in a small town in northern Minnesota, the "Land of 10,000 Lakes." I still love to fish streams in summer and go ice fishing in winter. I student taught in Minneapolis before moving here this year. This will be my first year teaching for the Maplewood School District—and my first year teaching ever!

I have planned an exciting year for my students. With the special assistance of my instructional aide, Mrs. Miller, we will continue the successful schoolwide reading program with a goal for each student to read and report on at least one free-reading book a month. Sixth-graders throughout the district will participate in a "Math Olympics Day."

Our students will also create exhibits for the annual Spring Science Fair. In social studies, we will study world geography, and students will each report in-depth on a country. (Your child will invite you to our international banquet at the end of the project.) I will keep you updated on all of these events and more with a monthly newsletter.

As a parent, you are the most important person in your child's life, and we need to work together for your child's benefit. I need your support for the homework assignments, academic goals and classroom discipline plan I have set for the students. I will keep you informed about your child's progress. With school and home working together, I know your child can have a successful year.

I look forward to meeting you personally at Back-to-School Night on September 30.

Sincerely,

Robert Marquez

Mr. Robert Marquez

Weekly Communication Folders

Once you have introduced yourself and your goals, make home-school communication part of your routine. Prepare a folder for each student and a letter telling parents what to expect.

What to Tell Parents About the Folder

☐ Their child will bring this folder home weekly.

☐ You will include a brief update about what the class has been studying.

☐ The folders will include student work samples.

☐ To encourage parents to comment on their children's work, let them know that you will include a space (or a page) for parent replies. Ask parents to review the folders and return them the next week.

Student Assignment Booklets

Use student assignment booklets for middle or secondary students. The booklets are filled in daily by the student, and parents can watch the books for teacher comments about progress.

Candid-Grams

Your students may forget to take home their homework, but they'll seldom forget to take home a candid compliment from the teacher. Use the "Teacher-Parent Telegram" and the "Parent-Teacher Telegram" in the resource section at the end of this chapter to send spontaneous messages about the student, to reinforce the student's sense that the teacher and parent "are in it together." Send home several copies of the latter form. When the parent initiates contact, send your reply the next day. When you initiate contact, request that the parents reply, even if it's just to say that they received the message.

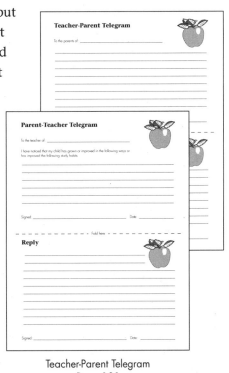

Teacher-Parent Telegram
Page 101

Parent-Teacher Telegram
Page 102

Activity Idea:
Parent Appreciation Station

Foster good relationships between students and their parents by raising students' awareness of their parents' contributions to their lives and learning.

Set up a Parent Appreciation Station before back-to-school night or open house. Make copies of the "Parent Appreciation Award" reproducible in the resource section. Place the awards at the station. Hold a class discussion about the various ways parents support their children—by helping with homework, providing extra care during an illness, planning family outings or dinners, working hard to support the family, and understanding when things go wrong.

Invite students to visit the Parent Appreciation Station whenever they have a moment and fill out a blank award. Use the awards to decorate the Parent Appreciation Station before the event.

Parent Appreciation Award
Page 103

Invite Volunteerism

Seeing a parent in the classroom lets a student sense that support for learning comes from home as well as from school. Today's parents often seem so busy that teachers hesitate to ask for help with field trips and classroom activities. If you feel reluctant to ask, simply send out a note that asks for a "raise of hands." A parent or two just might surprise you. Put out a call for volunteers using the reproducible "Please Lend a Helping Hand" form in the resource section. Place one on each desk at back-to-school night so parents who choose to volunteer will know of your needs. You may also send blank forms home with students before an event, field trip or project.

Please Lend a Helping Hand
Page 104

Plan Positive Phone Calls

When is the right time to call a parent? How about now? If the phone call is positive, just about any time is the right time.

Many parents hear from teachers only when their child has a problem. Imagine how surprised a parent will feel to receive a call from a teacher about something the student did *right*. The parents will pass on the compliment and add their own congratulations. The student who receives this extra reinforcement will feel encouraged to repeat the positive behavior or performance.

Start out the year by calling each student's parents and letting them know that you are eager to teach their child. Then make a habit of calling parents with positive reports from time to time. These occasions all present opportunities for a positive phone call:

- Before the first day of the school year, call to introduce yourself, express enthusiasm about your plans for the class and ask for information about the student.

- Call when a student performs a positive behavior, such as befriending a new student or helping you clean up the classroom after school.

- Call when a student applies himself or herself to an especially challenging task.

- Call when a student who has had difficulty in one area shows improvement.

- Call when a student is absent for more than a day or two, to say that the class missed him and to see whether the student needs work sent home.

A note to secondary school teachers: Don't let the large number of students you teach deter you from making positive contact with parents. Planning well will help you establish contact with every parent. You'd be surprised at the number of students you can reach if you just schedule time for positives. A quick positive phone call, for example, takes only a couple of minutes. Make two brief calls each afternoon and you will reach ten parents a week. Multiply that by 36 weeks and you will reach 360 parents. Think about when you could schedule time for calls each week. Then set a goal of speaking with a specific number of parents each week.

What to Say When You Call

Make a positive call similar to the one described below. Make a notation of anything the parent says that will help you support the student's positive behavior or performance. Commit to a schedule until you have contacted every student's parents.

Sample Positive Phone Conversation

Teacher: Mrs. Burris, this is Ms. Endicott, Charles's math teacher. I just wanted to let you know how well Charles is doing in school. He is a really hard worker. He gets right to work on all of his assignments, follows directions beautifully and always seems to do the best job he can.

Parent: Well, he does seem to like school more this year.

Teacher: I'm glad to hear that. I really enjoy having him in my classroom.

Parent: I appreciate your telling me this. It's really made my day!

Teacher: Well, I believe it's just as important to tell parents when their child is doing well in school as it is to tell parents when the child has a problem.

Parent: That makes sense to me.

Teacher: It makes sense to me too. There's one last thing. Please let Charles know that I called and how happy I am about how well he's doing in class. I want to be sure he knows that we notice and appreciate his good work.

Parent: I sure will! Thank you!

Use E-Mail and the Fax

At the beginning of the year, be sure to request parents' e-mail addresses and fax numbers in addition to phone numbers. When phone calls or face-to-face conferences are not convenient for either you or the parents to discuss issues relevant to their child, use e-mail messages or transmit information by fax. Many parents appreciate the direct line of communication and the immediacy these methods offer.

Confidently Communicate Problems

Your positive phone calls and positive written communication will help you establish a good relationship with parents, but eventually you may have to make less pleasant calls concerning a student's behavior or performance.

You may feel reluctant to initiate a conversation about a problem. You may wonder at what point a problem warrants a call. Many situations present an obvious need for a call: severe fighting, extreme emotional distress, refusal to perform schoolwork or an unusual change in behavior. In these circumstances, don't hesitate to call. Most parents, in fact, would want you to notify them before a problem becomes serious. But what about the day-to-day instances that seem less obvious? To decide whether to call on these occasions, use the "your own child" test:

1. Assume you have a child of your own the same age as the student in question.

2. If your child had the same problem in school that your student has, would you want the teacher to call you?

3. If the answer is yes, call the parent. If the answer is no, do not call the parent.

Please Note: While most parents probably share your philosophies about how to help a child improve his or her behavior, anticipate that some parents might administer harsher consequences than you feel a situation warrants. Exercise good judgment in deciding how and when to approach these parents about their children's behavior. Consult with your guidance counselor if you suspect that a parent might physically or mentally abuse a child, and report evidence of abuse to the proper authorities.

Once you decide that you need to contact a parent about a problem, a phone call is the most immediate way to communicate. It also allows you to clarify the problem and answer the parent's questions. Before you make the call, sit down and outline what you will say. To script your call, use the "Problem-Solving Phone Call Planner" in the resource section. For help, refer to the "What to Say When You Call About a Problem" guidelines on the next page. Your notes will provide a script for the call. They will also serve as a document that may prove important for your follow-up efforts throughout the year.

Project a positive, sensitive attitude. Keep in mind that you are not calling to place blame or to complain. You are calling because you care about the student's well-being and success at school.

Problem-Solving Phone Call Planner

Date of Call _____
Student's Name _____ Grade/Class: _____
Parent or Guardian _____
Home Phone _____ Work Phone _____

Jot down points you want to cover in each of these areas during the call.

Statement of concern _____

Describe the specific problem or behavior: _____

Describe steps you've taken so far: _____

Get parent input on the problem: _____
Record parent's comments: _____

Present ideas for solutions:
• What you'll do at school _____
• What you'd like the parent to do at home _____

Reassure the parent the problem can be solved: _____

Describe the followup contact the parent can expect _____
Notes: _____

Problem-Solving Phone Call Planner
Page 105

What to Say When You Call About a Problem

Keep the following objectives in mind as you plan your call:

1. **Begin with a statement of sincere concern.**

   Your introductory statement will set the tone for the conversation, so carefully phrase your remarks. Rather than saying, "Ms. Meyer, I'm calling because I am not pleased with Morgan's behavior," say, "Ms. Meyer, I'm calling because I'm concerned about how Morgan gets along with other students."

2. **Describe the specific behavior that necessitated the call.**

   Tell the parent in observable terms what the student did or did not do. Describe the behavior (such as hitting, shouting, or refusing to participate) and the number of times the problem has occurred. Rather than saying, "Morgan treats others cruelly," say, "Morgan hit three students over the course of the day."

3. **Describe steps you have taken to solve the problem.**

   Let the parent know that you are not calling in lieu of solving the problem yourself. Explain specifically what you have done to address the problem. "Last week I discussed the rule with her and I had her write down a commitment not to hit other students. Today, I sent her to the principal's office and later spoke with the principal about how to help her address this problem."

4. **Get information from the parent.**

   Ask for any information he or she can add that might help solve the problem. Listen to what the parent has to say to discover what may be troubling the student and exacerbating the behavior.

5. **Present your solutions to the problem.**

   Prepare to tell the parent exactly what you will do and what you would like the parent to do. Ask the parent to let the child know that you called and that both you and the parent feel concern about the problem.

6. **Express confidence in your ability to address the problem.**

   The parent may feel anxious and want to know that you have the ability to work with the child to correct the problem, just as a mother would want to know that a pediatrician could make her child well. Rather than saying, "I don't know how to handle this but I'll try," say, "Don't worry. Other students have had this problem. We can help Morgan."

7. **Plan for follow-up contact.**

   Promise the parent that you will follow up on this conversation. Commit to follow-up contact. Say, "I will contact you on Friday and let you know how things went."

Know How to Handle Hostile Confrontations

You may occasionally have to deal with angry or verbally aggressive parents. Practice your response by role-playing a meeting with such a parent. Ask a mentor or another colleague to take the part of the parent.

Steps for Defusing a Hostile Confrontation

1. Remain calm and thank the parent for expressing concern.
2. Listen to the parent's complaints without defending yourself or justifying your actions.
3. Show empathy and concern by asking the parent for more specific information.
4. Restate the student's problem behavior and clarify why it is not in his or her best interest to act this way.
5. If a parent still seems critical or angry, point out that it is in the child's best interest that you both work together toward a solution.
6. Finally, if the parent is still upset, suggest that he or she talk with the principal.

By practicing these steps, if you do have a confrontation with a parent, you can meet the situation with confidence and move toward a productive outcome.

Form Family Homework Partnerships

When you assign homework at the end of the day, the question of whether the homework comes back or not depends partly on the parents. Parents can serve as your most effective partners in ensuring that students complete their work efficiently, on time and in a way that reinforces classroom learning. Family learning projects can generate enthusiasm for your content. Helping parents fulfill their role as effective homework partners starts with a few basic actions on your part.

First, send a letter to communicate your expectations to parents at the beginning of the year. Explain how you would like them to become involved. Let them know how they can support their child in fulfilling homework responsibilities without actually doing the work for the child. The letter home should:

- Explain why you assign homework and describe the benefits for students.
- Explain the types of homework you will assign.

- Inform parents of the amount and frequency of the homework. Include the days of the week that you will assign homework and the amount of time you expect a student will need to complete it.

- Provide guidelines for when and how students should complete the homework. Include the relative importance of neatness, turning in the work in on time, and making up homework after an absence.

- Explain how homework will affect students' grades.

- Inform parents if you plan to give regularly scheduled tests on a certain day of the week.

- Let parents know how you will reinforce student's efforts to complete their homework. Also explain the consequences for not completing homework.

- Clarify what you expect of the parent.

Most parents want very much to ensure that their child completes his or her homework. They will probably appreciate the extra time you take to keep them informed and help them play a supportive role. The "Sample Homework Policy Letters" on the next two pages offer ideas for communicating a homework policy. Then use the "Homework Policy Planner" worksheet in the resource section to create your own policy.

Homework Policy Planner
Page 106

Define How You Will Process Homework

Once students and parents do their part, the teacher must follow up. You may feel overwhelmed with the task of assigning, assessing and returning homework. However, if you believe that the assignment is important enough for students to complete and turn in on time, your timely feedback is just as essential. The more thorough and immediate your responses, the more the homework will enhance student learning. To keep the process flowing, clearly define the procedures for processing homework.

- Determine an efficient procedure for collecting homework and recording the results. You may decide to have a student collect the assignments and to use an aide, a volunteer, or a student to help you record completed assignments and any grades or comments. Or you may assign cubbies or boxes where students turn in work.

- Determine and set expectations for what percentage of homework will apply toward grades. Not all homework needs to be graded, but students must know that homework will be checked and commented upon. To produce the best results, comment in a positive way, not just with general comments such as "good job" but with specific feedback.

- Decide on the options for correcting the work. Written work or big projects warrant detailed teacher comments, but straightforward worksheets or math problems present opportunities for students to correct each other's work. Consider setting up procedures for students to correct their own work or to correct each other's work. This gives the class an opportunity to discuss an assignment as a group or with another student.

Sample Homework Policy Letter
Elementary

Room 6 Homework Policy

To the Parents of _____ :

Why I Assign Homework: I believe homework is important because it is a valuable aid in helping students make the most of their experience in school. I give homework because it is useful in reinforcing what has been learned in class, prepares students for upcoming lessons, teaches responsibility and helps students develop positive study habits.

When I Assign Homework: Homework will be assigned Monday through Thursday nights. Assignments should take students no more than one hour to complete each night, not including studying for tests and working on projects. Spelling tests will be given each Friday. I will give students at least one week's notice to study for all tests, and one written report will be assigned each grading period.

Students' Homework Responsibilities: I expect students to do their best job on their homework. I expect homework to be neat, not sloppy. I expect students to do the work on their own and only ask for help after they have given it their best effort. I expect that all assignments will be turned in on time.

Teacher's Homework Responsibilities: I will check all homework and return it in a timely manner. Because I strongly believe in the value positive support plays in motivating children to develop good study habits, I will give students encouragement, and offer helpful feedback when they do their homework.

Parents' Homework Responsibilities: Parents play an important role in making homework a positive experience for their children. Therefore, I ask that parents make homework a top priority, provide necessary supplies and a quiet homework environment, set a daily homework time, provide praise and support, not let children avoid homework, and contact me if they notice a problem.

If Students Do Not Complete Homework: If students choose not to do their homework, I will talk with them to make sure they understand the assignment. If the problem persists, I will contact the parents to discuss possible solutions.

Please read and discuss this homework policy with your child. Then sign the bottom portion of this letter and return it to school.

Mrs. Roland

- -

I have read this homework policy and have discussed it with my child.

_____   _____
              Parent's Signature   Student's Signature

_____
              Date

Sample Homework Policy Letter
Secondary

Dear Parents,

I have written this letter to address questions you may have about homework assigned in my class. Please discuss the letter with your child and return the bottom portion.

Reason for Assigning Homework: Homework is a valuable tool in helping students make the most of their experience in school. Homework helps reinforce what has been learned in class, prepares students for upcoming lessons, teaches responsibility and helps students develop positive study habits.

When Homework Will Be Assigned: Homework will be assigned Monday through Thursday nights and occasionally on weekends. Homework should take no more than 45 minutes to complete, not including studying for mid-terms and finals. Students should read at least 15 minutes nightly in a library book of their choice. Book reports will be due in November, February and May.

Student's Homework Responsibilities: I expect students to do their best on each assignment. Homework should be neat, not sloppy. Daily written work should be completed in pencil. All reports should be written in ink, typed or computer generated. Homework should be finished by class time the following day.

Teacher's Homework Responsibilities: I will check all homework assignments and record them in my grade book. I will support good homework habits by giving praise and other incentives.

Parent's Homework Responsibilities: To make homework a positive experience, give it top priority at home, provide necessary supplies and a quiet environment, set aside a time every day to do homework, provide praise and positive support, help your child get to the library when necessary, do not allow your child to avoid doing homework, and contact me if you notice a problem.

Incomplete Homework: If students choose not to do homework, I will ask parents to begin checking and signing completed homework nightly. If the problem persists, students will lose certain privileges. After three homework assignments are incomplete or not turned in, the parent will be contacted. If students have a legitimate reason for not completing an assignment, please send me a signed note stating the reason.

Thanks for your support.

Mr. Tanaka

- -

I have read and discussed this homework policy with my child.

_____   _____
              Parent's Signature   Student's Signature

_____
              Date

Preview Next Week's Homework

At the beginning of each week, give parents a glimpse of the school week ahead. Preview the lessons, tests, assignments, assemblies, school holidays, and special events of the upcoming week on the "Sneak Preview" reproducible in the resource section. This regular update serves as an excellent parent/child communication tool. Suggest to parents that they ask their children about events and activities listed on the sheet during family discussions.

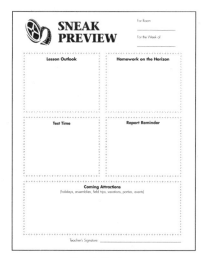

Sneak Preview
Page 107

Long-Term Assignments: Simplify and Notify

Parents dread finding out at the last minute that their child has a big project—due tomorrow! You can help them avoid this scenario by informing parents at the beginning of a long-term project and keeping them updated throughout the process.

Keep long-term assignments (reports, papers, projects) on track and keep parents informed by:

- Sending home a detailed description of the project.

- Having students tackle long-term assignments by completing one phase at a time. Provide due dates for specific stages of the project (outline, first draft, final copy).

- Writing detailed comments on the papers you send home, when feasible. Parents will appreciate your positive comments and objective reviews, and students will better understand your expectations for the *next* long-term project.

Boost Students' Study Skills

Help older students take responsibility for improving their study habits by distributing the "Study Tips" reproducible in the resource section. You can include this sheet in a parent handbook you compile for back-to-school night (see page 96) or give it directly to students.

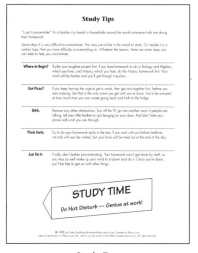

Study Tips
Page 108

Homework Correspondence Idea:
Send an "S.O.S."

Inform parents when homework problems arise by attaching these attention-getting notices to incomplete or unacceptable homework assignments.

Reproduce the "S.O.S." notes in the resource section on bright yellow paper, cut apart and keep in an envelope inside your grade book or homework log. As you record homework information (assignments turned in, grades, comments), fill in S.O.S. notes to alert parents of homework problems such as:

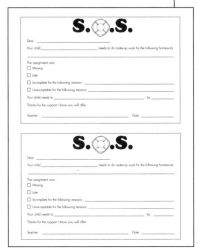

S.O.S.
Page 109

- Missing assignments.

- Late assignments.

- Unacceptable assignments (sloppy, inaccurate, illegible, incomplete).

When parents receive an S.O.S. note, they should discuss the problem with their child and make sure the child completes the homework. The S.O.S. note should be signed by the parent and returned to school attached to the homework assignment.

Middle School Idea:
Let Students Alert Parents

It may be unrealistic for middle school teachers to notify parents each time a student misses an assignment. Instead, encourage accountability by asking students to monitor their own assignments.

- Write the week's assignments on the board and ask students to copy down the assignment calendar for the week each Monday.

- If students have not turned in all their work on time during the week, then have students write a letter to their parents on the following Monday explaining what work they did not complete, the reasons for the missed work and their plans for completing their work in the coming week.

Enhance Learning at Home

A parent's efforts to enhance learning can include homework help, reading time, and everyday activities. You can probably dream up a hundred ways to include parents as partners in the learning process. The resources in this section will highlight just a few of them.

Review the reproducibles and select the ones that best serve your families and support your curriculum. Customize them as needed or simply reproduce them. Distribute these reproducibles at timely intervals throughout the year to correspond with your classroom activities. Or compile them in a handbook to pass out at back-to-school night. See page 96 for more suggestions about what to include in a parent handbook.

3

Ten Helpful Homework Hints
to Use with Your Child
Page 110

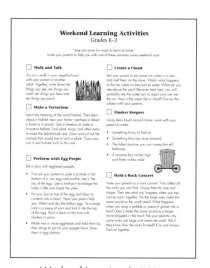

Weekend Learning Activities
Pages 111–113

How Can I Help My Child
Succeed in School?
Page 114

Recommended Children's Books
Pages 115–118

Shared Reading Time Activities
Page 119

Communicate with Non-English-Speaking Parents

Today's diverse classrooms present new challenges for teachers. From urban centers to rural communities, teachers now face classrooms with some students whose primary language is not English. Many school districts have developed English-as-a-Second-Language (ESL) or English Language Learning (ELL) programs, but some states continue to debate whether to teach children through immersion or provide bilingual classrooms. Regardless of how quickly children learn a second language, they generally learn it more quickly than their parents, whose linguistic patterns developed long ago.

If you speak a second language, you will probably find it an asset in dealing with non-English-speaking parents. If you do not, you may want to take advantage of the resources available to you. Your school may provide written communications in the languages prevalent in your school community. Your school district may also provide ESL or ELL trainers, aides or volunteers who can help you translate oral and written communication to parents. If you do not have access to these resources, you may want to ask an older student to interpret during a conference with parents. You can also access Web sites that offer free translations. The translations are literal, so use a straightforward writing style without idioms and have a person who speaks the language check the translations for meaning. Imagine inputting a parent letter, pushing a few keys, and printing out an instant translation! As the challenges increase, so does the technology that can help you meet them.

Web Resources for Working with
Non-English-Speaking Parents
Page 120

Copy the "Web Resources for Working with Non-English-Speaking Parents" reproducible in the resource section. Share it with other teachers. Please note that the site addresses fluctuate from time to time. If the site you need is no longer in service, conduct an Internet search for a similar site. Key in "translation" and then the language into which you wish to translate.

Make Back-to-School Night Memorable

Back-to-school night presents a great opportunity to establish a collaborative relationship with parents, but only if you first build participation. Unfortunately, not all parents attend back-to-school night, perhaps because past events were not informative or because of parents' reluctance to come to school.

Set a goal for 100% back-to-school attendance. Ensure a great turnout and a worthwhile experience by sending home invitations that "sell" the event and explain the benefits for parents. For example, if time permits, videotape students as they go about projects or make presentations and interview students on camera. Advertise this special video presentation in your invitation. If a taped presentation is not possible, you may want to present a student-created diorama or art exhibit.

Make it easy for parents to attend. Ask your administration if child care will be available and promote this feature. Ask for R.S.V.P.s on the invitation and call parents who do not plan to attend. Send home materials that they might miss by not attending. Copy or customize the "Please Come to Back-to-School Night" or the "You're Invited to Back to School Night" reproducible in the resource section for your own use.

Once parents arrive in your classroom, make sure you let them feel welcome and give them a good feeling about their children's experience in your classroom. Keep these pointers in mind:

- Work from a planned outline when addressing parents. Remain enthusiastic as you introduce yourself, your curriculum plans and your discipline and homework policies.

- Let parents know how they can help. Leave plenty of time for questions. Take notes if parents make suggestions so you can follow up later with a phone call or written note. Tell them how they can contact you. Assure them that you want to hear about their concerns.

- Consider giving a slide presentation to show students working on classroom activities, or play an audiotape or videotape of students discussing their classroom activities and projects. Make sure you include every member of the class in the slides or on the tape.

- Have each student leave a note written to his or her parents. The parents may read the note and write a return message that the student will find the next morning.

- Display samples of student work on bulletin boards, on tables and at desks.

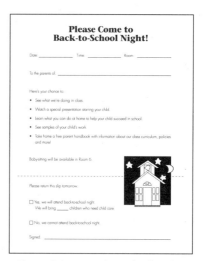

Please Come to Back-to-School Night! (Elementary) Page 121

You're Invited to Back-to-School Night (Secondary) Page 122

- Explain how you use volunteers in your class and extend an invitation for parents to help out with special projects you have planned.

- Distribute a parent handbook or a folder of useful information as well as resources to help parents support their children's learning. (See the suggestions below.) Make sure that all parents receive this information, even those who cannot attend.

- A few days after back-to-school night, follow up with a thank-you note to parents who attended and an update for those who did not. Include follow-up formation on your presentation and responses to specific parent questions.

Suggested Elements
of Parent Handbook

☐ Class list

☐ Staff list

☐ School address, phone number and school hours

☐ A note about yourself

☐ A daily classroom schedule

☐ Grade level curriculum information

☐ Your homework policy

☐ Your discipline policy

☐ School calendar

☐ Policies about absences, medical appointments and make-up work

☐ Health concerns

Include reproducibles from this section:

☐ Parent-Teacher Telegrams

☐ Please Lend a Helping Hand

☐ Study Tips

☐ Ten Helpful Homework Hints to Use with Your Child

☐ Weekend Learning Activities

☐ How Can I Help My Child Succeed in School?

☐ Recommended Children's Books

☐ Shared Reading Time Activities

Tackle Conference-Time Jitters

Many new teachers report feeling nervous the first time they conduct parent conferences. Knowing what to say can intimidate even veteran teachers. Yet regularly scheduled conferences can help you teach more effectively. They can help strengthen your partnership with parents, give them a general overview of their child's progress, and help you address any concerns they might have. Talking with the parents can give you new insight into the student's thinking.

By conference time, you may have already have made positive contact with parents. The conference will enable you to conduct a more in-depth discussion about their child. Find out when your school schedules parent conferences and plan ahead to solicit parent support.

The following steps will help you feel more prepared and confident, will help the parents gain valuable information about their child, and will enhance the productive nature of the conference:

- Send home the reproducible "Parent Conference Invitation" provided in the resource section. Include a personalized note. Explain the purpose of the conference. Emphasize the positive nature of the conference in case some parents assume the purpose is to discuss problems.

- Offer parents flexible time choices. Give them as options and include a detachable portion of the invitation that they can return to you. Fill in the appropriate dates before reproducing the invitation.

- Prepare for the conferences by putting together samples of each student's class work. Use the work to help you illustrate statements you might make regarding the student's performance in class.

- Fill out a "Parent Conference Planning Sheet" for each student before the conference, using the reproducible provided in the resource section. Because each conference is brief, you will want to make the most of your time. Write down in advance all the issues you plan to discuss. Keep the sheet in front of you so you can record the parents' comments. Keep the document in the student's file or portfolio.

Parent Conference Invitation
Page 123

Parent Conference Planning Sheet
Page 124

- On the day of the conference, try to make the setting as comfortable as possible. Arrange to have adult-sized chairs in your room. Give some thought to the comfort of parents as they wait their turn. Place two chairs outside the door along with a stack of student textbooks and workbooks for parents to preview.

- Greet parents enthusiastically and set a warm, caring tone for the conference. Treat them as you would want to be treated. Since the parent is a guest and you are a host, it's your responsibility to make the experience pleasurable, productive and informative.

- Follow the guidelines on your planning sheet, but save ample time for parents to express themselves. Your ability to listen will prove just as important as your ability to inform. If a parent seems negative, confused, or hostile, see it as an opportunity to earn the parent's support. Some parents have had experiences that left them with an unfavorable reaction to school. One teacher's commitment and enthusiasm could change the picture for them—and for their child. If language barriers present a problem, offer to supply an interpreter.

- Schedule telephone conferences for parents unable to attend a face-to-face parent-teacher conference. Offer to supply an interpreter, if necessary.

Spread the Welcome Mat at Open House

While back-to-school night usually involves information sessions for parents, presented by teachers, open house, which usually occurs later in the year, gives your students a chance to share information and student work. Encourage them to show parents their work and the highlights of their home-away-from-home. Offer a warm welcome to both students and parents and make this an opportunity to celebrate the students' learning. The following steps will help.

Create Special Invitations

Even if your school sends out notices to each family, have your students write personal invitations. Ask them to tell their parents about several items they particularly want to share. If you like, have them mention these items on the "Open House Invitation" reproducible in the resource section.

Plan Ahead

Keep some student projects so you can exhibit them at open house. Let students participate in choosing their best work to display on a bulletin board or in the hallway, or to share in portfolios left out on their desks. Give each student a "Classroom Tour" worksheet provided in the resource section to fill out and use as they escort their parents through the room. The more students feel engaged in the planning, the more enthusiastically they will share their work with their parents. Prepare a sign-in sheet for parents, to make it easier to send thank-you notes to those who attended.

Creatively Showcase Student Work

Show your students "in action" during the year. Draw on some of the following ideas:

- Present a slide show or create a bulletin board featuring highlights from field trips and class presentations. Depict students engaged in positive behaviors or memorable activities. You may want to involve students in taking pictures early in the year for this purpose.

- Have students share their computer work on disks or CD-ROMs. Make computers available in the room so families can access the work.

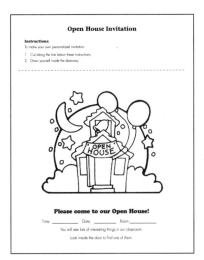

Open House Invitation
Page 125

Classroom Tour
Page 126

- Show a video of students giving presentations to the class.
- Cover windows, doors and walls with student work. Suspend artwork from the ceiling.
- Cover a table with class books, a class photo album and student portfolios.
- Create a label for each display in the room. For instance, "Memory Lane" can include class scrapbooks or photos. "Hall of Fame" could designate a bulletin board displaying awards and student recognition.
- Set up a hands-on science experiment the whole family can try.

You've learned some ideas for continual correspondence, positive phone calls, addressing problems and planning parent events. Look for other opportunities throughout the year for parents to celebrate their children's learning. When you open the door to parents, you encourage a much greater level of success and well-being among your students.

Honor Parents at Year's End

Occasional notes of appreciation can have a lasting effect on students and parents, especially parting notes sent at the end of the year. Take a few minutes to write a heartfelt, encouraging message to each student and parent in your class. For ideas, see the following example of a parting letter to parents.

Sample Note to Parents

Dear Mr. and Mrs. Juma,

This year has been very successful for Mike, and I hope you realize the important part you played in that success. By scheduling homework into his routine, Mike was able to excel in his schoolwork as well as in his gymnastics. Thank you for encouraging him both in his studies and his sports. Have a wonderful summer. I look forward to seeing you at school events next year.

Mr. Patel

Teacher-Parent Telegram

To the parents of: _____

_____

_____

_____

_____

_____

_____

_____

_____

Signed: _____ Date: _____

- - - - - - - - - - - - Fold here - - - - - - - - -

Reply

_____

_____

_____

_____

_____

_____

_____

_____

_____

Signed: _____ Date: _____

Parent-Teacher Telegram

To the teacher of: _____

I have noticed that my child has grown or improved in the following ways or has improved the following study habits:

_____

_____

_____

_____

_____

_____

Signed: _____ Date: _____

- - - - - - - - - - - - Fold here - - - - - - - - - - - -

Reply

_____

_____

_____

_____

_____

_____

_____

_____

_____

Signed: _____ Date: _____

Parent Appreciation Award

Dear _____,

Remember when _____
_____?

I do and I just want to say, "Thanks!"

Love, _____

Parent Appreciation Award

Dear _____,

Remember when _____
_____?

I do and I just want to say, "Thanks!"

Love, _____

Please Lend a Helping Hand

Dear Parent,

Our class could use an extra pair of hands. We hope you can volunteer.

Here's what we need:

_____

_____

_____

_____

_____ _____ _____
Signed   Date   Room#

Cut here and return to school.

- -

I can help.

☐   I'd be happy to lend a hand. You can count on me to:

_____

_____

_____

_____

☐   Thank you for asking, but I will not
     be able to help out this time.
     Please ask me again.

_____ _____ _____
Signed   Date   Phone

Problem-Solving Phone Call Planner

Date of Call: _____

Student's Name: _____ Grade/Class: _____

Parent or Guardian: _____

Home Phone: _____ Work Phone: _____

Jot down points you want to cover in each of these areas during the call.

Statement of concern: _____

_____

Describe the specific problem or behavior: _____

Describe steps you've taken so far: _____

_____

Get parent input on the problem: _____

Record parent's comments: _____

_____

Present ideas for solutions:

• What you'll do at school: _____

_____

• What you'd like the parent to do at home: _____

_____

Reassure the parent the problem can be solved: _____

_____

Describe the follow-up contact the parent can expect: _____

Notes: _____

_____

_____

_____

Homework Policy Planner

Use this form as a planner when you
develop your Homework Policy.

Why do you assign homework?

_____

_____

What are the types of homework you will assign?

_____

_____

How often will you assign homework? How long should the assignments take?

_____

_____

What guidelines will you give students for completing homework?

_____

_____

What are the students' responsibilities in the homework process?

_____

_____

What are the responsibilities of parents in the homework process?

_____

_____

What are the teacher's responsibilities?

_____

_____

How will homework affect a student's grade?

_____

_____

Now use the information on this sheet to write your homework policy letter to parents.

SNEAK PREVIEW

For Room

_____

For the Week of

_____

Lesson Outlook

Homework on the Horizon

Test Time

Report Reminder

Coming Attractions
(holidays, assemblies, field trips, vacations, parties, events)

Teacher's Signature: _____

Study Tips

"I can't concentrate!" It's a familiar cry heard in households around the world whenever kids are doing their homework.

Some days it is very difficult to concentrate. You may just not be in the mood to study. Or maybe it is a certain topic that you have difficulty concentrating on. Whatever the reason, there are some steps you can take to help you concentrate.

Where to Begin?	Tackle your toughest project first. If you have homework to do in Biology and Algebra, which you love, and History, which you hate, do the History homework first. Your mind will be fresher and you'll get through it quicker.
Got Pizza?	If you keep having the urge to get a snack, then get one together first, before you start studying. But that is the only snack you get until you're done. You'd be amazed at how much time you can waste going back and forth to the fridge.
Shhh.	Remove any other distractions. Turn off the TV, go into another room if people are talking, tell your little brother to quit banging on your door. And don't take any phone calls until you are through.
Think Early.	Try to do your homework early in the day. If you wait until just before bedtime, not only will you be rushed, but your brain will be tired out at the end of the day.
Just Do It.	Finally, don't bother procrastinating. Your homework won't get done by itself, so you may as well make up your mind to sit down and do it. Once you're done, you'll be free to get on with other things.

STUDY TIME
Do Not Disturb — Genius at work!

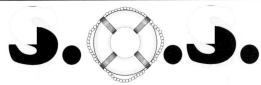

Dear: _____

Your child_____ needs to do make-up work for the following homework:

_____

The assignment was:

☐ Missing

☐ Late

☐ Incomplete for the following reasons: _____

☐ Unacceptable for the following reasons: _____

Your child needs to _____ by _____

Thanks for the support I know you will offer.

Teacher: _____ Date: _____

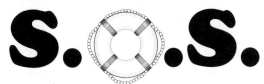

Dear: _____

Your child_____ needs to do make-up work for the following homework:

_____

The assignment was:

☐ Missing

☐ Late

☐ Incomplete for the following reasons: _____

☐ Unacceptable for the following reasons: _____

Your child needs to _____ by _____.

Thanks for the support I know you will offer.

Teacher: _____ Date: _____

Ten Helpful Homework Hints to Use with Your Child

1. **Convey to your child your expectations about homework.** Your consistent message should be: "Homework is important to your success in school, and I expect homework to be done appropriately." It is critical that your child understands that you place as much importance on homework being done each night as you do on your child going to school each day.

2. **Set aside a special time each night just for homework.** Most of your child's sports activities, music lessons and doctor visits are scheduled. Add homework to the schedule. Decide with your child on an appropriate time for doing homework each night.

3. **Set up a proper study area.** Experts agree that a quiet study environment is a must. Make sure your child has a desk or table in a quiet place, and insist that all homework is done there.

4. **Create a "homework survival kit."** Minimize time lost when your child is looking for items necessary for completing assignments. Put together a "homework survival kit"—a box that holds critical supplies such as paper, sharpened pencils, eraser, markers, ruler, folders, glue and index cards.

5. **Decide on a "homework drop spot."** Avoid morning hunts for missing homework assignments by choosing a place where your child puts all completed assignments the night before and picks them up in the morning.

6. **Show interest in your child's assignments.** When your child shows you completed assignments, take time to look at them, ask questions and show support by offering specific comments: "This is an excellent map you've drawn. It shows every detail."

7. **Offer praise as motivation.** Check assignments and offer well-deserved praise for the efforts your child makes. Your praise will motivate your child to keep up the good work.

8. **Call the teacher about homework concerns.** Very often the teacher can suggest a solution to a problem that might be bothering you or your child. By working together, you and the teacher can enhance the opportunity for your child to succeed in school.

9. **Use a "Homework Contract" if your child still has problems doing homework.** This contract is a written and signed agreement between you and your child that states: 1) the specific homework rule that must be followed, 2) the specific reward your child will receive for following the homework rule, and 3) the consequences that will occur if your child doesn't do homework appropriately.

10. **Stay involved and informed.** Check your child's list of assignments each night to make sure all homework is getting done, to stay involved with what's going on in class, to answer any questions your child may have, and to be alerted to any long-range assignments and tests.

Weekend Learning Activities
Grades K–3

Here are some fun ways to learn at home.
Invite your parents to help you with one of these activities some weekend soon.

☐ Walk and Talk

Go on a walk in your neighborhood with your parent or another adult. Together, write down ten things you see, ten things you smell, ten things you hear and ten things you touch.

☐ Make a Terrarium

Learn the meaning of the word habitat. Then learn about a habitat near your home—perhaps a desert, a forest or a prairie. Use a shoebox to make a miniature habitat. Find sand, twigs, and other items to make the habitat look real. Draw and cut out the animals that would live in such a place. If you can, visit a real habitat such as this one.

☐ Perform with Egg People

Tell a story with egghead puppets.

- First ask your parent to poke a pinhole in the bottom of a raw egg and another one in the top of the egg. Use a toothpick to enlarge the holes a little and break the yoke.

- Put your lips on top of the egg and blow its contents into a bowl. Have your parent help you. Wash and dry the hollow egg. Tie a large knot in a piece of yarn and tuck it into the top of the egg. Paint a face on the front with markers or paint.

- Make two or more eggheads and hold them by their strings to put on your puppet show. Store them in egg cartons.

☐ Create a Cloud

Ask your parent to put some ice cubes in a pan and melt them on the stove. Watch what happens to the ice cubes as they turn to water. What do you see above the pan? Because heat rises, you will probably see the water turn to vapor and rise into the air. How is the vapor like a cloud? Discuss the subject with your parents.

☐ Finders Keepers

Using items found around home, work with your parent to make:

- Something funny to look at.

- Something that can move forward.

- The tallest structure you can create that still balances.

- A structure four inches high and three inches wide.

☐ Hold a Rock Concert

Invite your parents to a rock concert. First collect all the rocks you can find. Group them by size and shape. Then see what you happens when you tap various rocks together. Do the large ones make the same sound as the small ones? What happens when you drop a pebble or piece of gravel into a box? Does it make the same sound as a larger stone dropped in the box? Ask your parents why some rocks are large and some are small. Ask if they know how the rocks formed? If no one knows, find out together.

Weekend Learning Activities
Grades 4–6

☐ Fry Up Some Fractions

Learn fractions by cooking with your parents. Choose a recipe that calls for cups or teaspoons. See how many ways you can end up with one cup (using a whole cup measure, a half-cup measure, a third-cup measure and a quarter-cup measure). Or try the same exercise with a teaspoon.

☐ Trash Tally

Hold an environmental awareness weekend. For two days, keep a notepad on the kitchen counter. Have family members write down each item they throw in the trash. At the end of the weekend, hold a family meeting to review the list and discuss what natural resources the family used. Base the discussion on questions such as the following:

- Were most of the items paper, aluminum or plastic?
- Did the discarded items come from trees?
- How many items went into a recycling bin? How many were biodegradable?
- Did family members throw away uneaten food at the end of each meal?

Discuss the environmental impact of one family's weekend trash. Did family members use natural resources wisely by recycling non-food items and by serving only as much food as they could eat? Have family members think of one habit they can change to help the environment.

☐ Smart Shopper

Go to the grocery store with your family. Pretend you have $25.00 to spend. Your job is to plan a lunch and dinner for four people. Make sure each meal is well balanced. Write down your menu and the cost of each item you will have to buy.

☐ Play the Categories Game

When riding in the car or spending an evening with your family, play this word game to test your knowledge of geography, wildlife, literature and other categories of information.

The first person chooses a category, for instance "countries," and says the name of a country, such as Kenya. The next person must think of a country that starts with the last letter of "Kenya"—A. If he or she says "Afghanistan," the next person might say, "Nicaragua."

Keep going around the circle until the players start to run out of words, then change categories. See the following examples for animals and books:

- Animals:

  Cougar...rat...tarantula...alligator...red-tailed hawk...kangaroo...ocelot...termite...egret.

- Books (do not count "The" as a word):

  The House at Pooh Corner...The Red Pony...The Yearling...Goldilocks and the Three Bears.

Weekend Learning Activities
Middle School

Historical Tour

When driving somewhere together with your family, look at the homes, businesses, schools, houses of worship and public buildings in your town or city. Discuss what they tell you about your community's history.

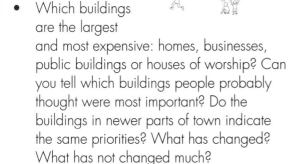

- Can you tell which part of town was built first?

- Why do you think the builders used the materials they chose?

- Which buildings are the largest and most expensive: homes, businesses, public buildings or houses of worship? Can you tell which buildings people probably thought were most important? Do the buildings in newer parts of town indicate the same priorities? What has changed? What has not changed much?

- Ask your parents or grandparents whether they can point out structures built at the turn of the 20th century, those built during the Great Depression (by the WPA), those built after World War II, those built between 1960 and 1980, and those built during your lifetime. Get their opinion on what the architecture reflects about the economy, customs and history during that period.

Plan a Road Trip

Help plan a road trip for your family. Whether your destination is 100 miles or 1,000 miles away, you can probably find historical or natural sights along the way that you never knew existed. Choose several ways to research the place you plan to visit:

- Go to a library or bookstore to look up your destination in the encyclopedias and travel books.

- Use a school or home computer to find Web-site information about the place you plan to visit.

- Write a letter to a chamber of commerce, park service or historical society of the nearest town.

- Collect maps and have your parents help you plan the route. Determine the time it will take to get there. Study the maps and find possible points of interest along the way. Research new information about those places.

- Ask your parents to let you help navigate by watching for landmarks along the way.

- Once you arrive, talk to the people you meet in stores and gas stations and ask the most interesting thing they think you should see while you're there. It may be a sight you did not read about in the books!

Speak Out!

Interview your parent to find out about

_____

Possible subjects:

- Your family tree.

- His or her opinion of the United Nations.

- His or her favorite book.

- What he or she would do in case of an emergency (such as an earthquake, tornado or flood).

- His or her opinion about the best place in the world to live.

There's no place like home.

How Can I Help My Child Succeed in School?

- Read aloud to your child. Research has proved that this is the most important thing a parent can do to ensure a child's reading progress.

- Have your child read to you.

- Read together: You read a sentence. Your child reads a sentence.

- Obtain a library card for your child and check out a book.

- Subscribe to child-oriented magazines. Read them together.

- Create flashcards for your child's particular needs—alphabet recognition, vocabulary words, numbers, math facts, states and capitals.

- Have your child follow a recipe, measure ingredients and prepare a dish.

- Have your child figure change from the grocery or department store.

- Help your child organize homework. Proofread the work with the child before the child turns it in.

- Celebrate your child's discoveries and let the child see your joy as you learn together.

Recommended Children's Books
Grades K–3

Give your child plenty of inspiring resources to fill his or her daily reading time.
This recommended children's fiction list offers many colorful, educational, character-building topics.

Catundra
S. Cosgrove
Price/Stern/Sloan

Other animals ridicule a tubby cat before an obliging mole becomes her personal trainer.

A Chair for My Mother
V. Williams
Greenwillow

When Rosa's house burns down, she unites with her mother and grandmother to save dimes so they can buy a chair.

The Giving Tree
S. Silverstein
Harpercollins Juvenile Books

A story about a tree willing to sacrifice everything for a young boy who takes the gifts for granted.

It Takes a Village
J. Cowen-Fletcher
Scholastic

In this story, West African Yemi almost loses her brother but her neighbors come to the rescue.

The Legend of the Bluebonnet
T. dePaola
Putnam

A Comanche heroine sacrifices her most prized possession to save her people from drought.

Love You Forever
S. McGraw
Firefly Books

A mother sings to her newborn son. This book captures the magic of the bond between parent and child.

The Meanest Thing to Say
B. Cosby
Cartwheel Books

A Bill Cosby classic. Little Bill "plays the dozens" with a bully. He finds a way to stop hurting his friend's feelings.

Milo and the Magical Stones
M. Pfister
North South Books

Milo the Mouse discovers a magic stone that he hopes will change life on his island.

Now One Foot, Now the Other
T. dePaola
Putnam

Bobby struggles to understand what has happened to his grandfather in the aftermath of a stroke. He discovers an opportunity to help his grandfather learn how to walk again.

The Patchwork Quilt
V. Flournoy
E.P. Dutton

Tanya's grandmother helps her make a family quilt, then becomes ill. Tanya is determined to finish.

Somewhere in Africa
I. Mennen & N. Daly
Puffin Books

Ashraf lives in Africa, but learns about African wildlife through books in the library.

Stellaluna
J. Cannon
Harcourt Brace

A baby fruit bat is separated from her mother and befriends a family of birds, who raise her in a most peculiar way.

Stone Soup
A. McGovern
Scholastic Trade

When an old woman can't feed a hungry young boy, he convinces her he can make soup with a stone.

The Treasure Hunt
B. Cosby
Cartwheel Books

Young Bill Cosby yearns for a special talent or passion. He thinks he has little to offer the world until his grandmother helps him discover his gift for storytelling.

The Velveteen Rabbit
M. Williams Bianco
Henry Holt

The classic story about a toy rabbit that becomes real through the love of a young boy.

White Wave
D. Wolkstein
Harcourt Brace

A young Chinese farmer discovers a goddess living in a snail shell. The shell transforms his life.

Recommended Children's Books
Grades 4–6

Give your child plenty of inspiring resources to fill his or her daily reading time.
This recommended children's fiction list offers many colorful, educational, character-building topics.

Brother Eagle, Sister Sky: A Message from Chief Seattle
S. Jeffers
Dial

Chief Seattle asks "How can you buy the sky?" in this wonderfully illustrated book.

The Cay
T. Taylor
Camelot

A 12-year old white boy and an old black man are stranded on a Caribbean island. The boy finds new vision, courage and respect for his companion.

Charlotte's Web
E.B. White
HarperTrophy

Determined to save her friend Wilbur the pig, Charlotte tries to convince everyone that Wilbur is no ordinary animal.

The Egypt Game
Z. Keatley-Snyder
Atheneum

April and Melanie both love Egypt. A deserted storage yard becomes their make-believe land, but strange things happen when they take their Egypt game too far.

The Friends
K. Yumoto
Farrar Strauss and Giroux

Three friends become pre-occupied with death after one of them attends a funeral. They observe an elderly neighbor to learn about death but, in the end, they learn about life.

Harriet the Spy
L. Fitzhugh
HarperTrophy

An intensely curious and intelligent girl spies on people and writes about them in her secret notebook, which is discovered by her classmates.

Indian in the Cupboard
L.R. Banks
Avon

A magic cupboard transforms a boy's plastic cowboys and Indians into actual miniature people.

Island of the Blue Dolphins
S. O'Dell
Yearling

Based on the real-life story of a young American-Indian girl who jumped ship to stay with her young brother on an abandoned island.

The Phantom Tollbooth
N. Juster
Random House

Milo travels to The Lands Beyond when he drives his small electric car through a mysterious, miniature tollbooth gate.

Sarah, Plain and Tall
P. MacLachlan
HarperTrophy

When Papa's new wife, Sarah, arrives from Maine, the children begin to love her but fear that she will one day leave them.

The Trumpet of the Swan
E.B. White
HarperTrophy

Louis the mute swan's determination allows him to become a great trumpet player, attract a mate and return to the wilderness.

To Walk the Skypath
P. Naylor
Yearling

A Seminole Indian boy becomes the first in his family to attend school. His curiosity about the white man's world competes with his commitment to fulfill his family's ancestral wishes.

Where the Red Fern Grows
W. Rawls
Bantam

A young boy's devotion to two hunting dogs teaches him qualities of maturity and responsibility.

A Wrinkle in Time
M. L'Engle
Farrar, Strauss and Giroux

Meg and her brother set out with a friend to find their missing father, traveling through space and time as an evil power darkens the cosmos.

Recommended Children's Books
Middle School

Give your child plenty of inspiring resources to fill his or her daily reading time.
This recommended children's fiction list offers many colorful, educational, character-building topics.

Are You There, God? It's Me, Margaret
J. Blume
Laurel Leaf Library

A young girl grapples with her inability to control the pace of puberty or to understand her increasingly complex relationship with God.

Baseball in April and Other Stories
G. Soto
Harcourt Brace

Eleven short stories describe day-to-day life in a contemporary Mexican-American community.

The Boys' War
J. Murphy
Clarion

A perspective on the Civil War, seen through the eyes of young boys, both Union and Confederate, who fought in it.

The Chocolate War
R. Cormier
Laureleaf

A high school freshman must examine his principles when a school candy sale turns into a gang war.

The Giver
L. Lowry
Laurel Leaf Library

A 12-year-old boy living in a utopian world becomes his community's "Receiver of Memories." He rethinks the value of giving up one's humanity for a perfect society.

Homecoming
C. Voight
Fawcett

Abandoned by their mother, four homeless siblings camp their way through Southern New England with inspiring resilience and resourcefulness.

Journey to Topaz
Y. Uchida
Creative Arts

Yuki spends Christmas of 1941 on her way to an internment camp. The book tells the story of the uprooting of Japanese Americans during World War II.

Lyddie
K. Paterson
Puffin

A young farm girl goes to work in a factory to pay debts incurred by her father, who left the family.

M.C. Higgins, the Great
V. Hamilton
Aladdin

A teenager tries to save his family's home from the encroachment of strip mining.

On My Honor
M.D. Bauer
Houghton Mifflin

Joel told his parents he would never go near the raging river. When his friend drowns, he must offer an explanation to both sets of parents.

Roll of Thunder, Hear My Cry
M. Taylor
Dial

A black family from Mississippi survives discrimination to defend their land, integrity and independence.

Sounder
W.H. Armstrong
Harpercollins

When a black sharecropper loses his freedom and his family, his son turns to a devoted dog for comfort.

To Kill a Mockingbird
H. Lee
Warner Books

A classic story of life in a small Southern town from the eyes of a young girl, Scout. The reader learns what it means to stand up to prejudice and injustice.

A Wrinkle in Time
M. L'Engle
Farrar, Strauss and Giroux

Meg and her brother set out with a friend to find their missing father, traveling through space and time as an evil power darkens the cosmos.

Yolanda's Genius
C. Fenner
Alladin Paperbacks

Yolanda can see the genius in her younger brother. She helps the world discover his gift for the Blues.

Recommended Books
High School

This recommended teen fiction list offers many colorful, educational, character-building topics.

Anne Frank the Diary of a Young Girl
A. Frank
Bantam Books

Anne and her family are Jews, who go into hiding in Nazi-occupied Amsterdam. Anne's diary about the experience was discovered after the war ended.

The Bell Jar
S. Plath
Harperennial Library

A vulnerable young girl wins a dream assignment on a big New York fashion magazine and finds herself in a terrifying descent toward madness.

The Best Little Girl in the World
S. Levenkron
Warner Books

Kessie, a teenage ballet dancer, thinks she's overweight. She's five foot four and ninety-eight pounds. Kessie has anorexia nervosa.

The Catcher in the Rye
J. Salinger
Little Brown & Company

Sixteen-year-old Holden Caulfield has just been expelled from prep school. Confused and disillusioned, he rails against the "phoniness" of the adult world.

The Chocolate War
R. Cormier
Laureleaf

A high school freshman must examine his principles when a school candy sale turns into a gang war.

Dead Poets Society
N. Kleinbaum
Bantam Books

An English teacher challenges Todd and his friends to "make your lives extraordinary!" The boys form a secret club where they let their passions run wild.

I Know Why the Caged Bird Sings
M. Angelou
Bantam Books

This autobiography traces poet Maya Angelou's childhood in a small, rural community during the 1930s.

Jacob I Have Loved
K. Paterson
HarperTrophy

Sara Louise, in a quest for self-knowledge, recalls her turbulent adolescence and her intense jealousy of her own twin sister.

Lord of the Flies
W. Golding
Perigee

An adventure tale of a group of English school boys marooned on an unpopulated island and who must confront the defects of their society and of their own natures.

The Outsiders
S. Hinton
Puffin

Ponyboy is 14, tough and confused, but also immensely sensitive. This is his touching story of friends, loyalty, violence and society.

The Pigman
P. Zindel
Bantam Books

Two lonely high school students befriend a strange old man. Mr. Pignati, the "Pigman," has a beer belly and an awful secret.

Something Wicked This Way Comes
R. Bradbury
Bantam Books

A carnival comes to town, and best friends Will and Jim confront a nightmarish evil that will change their lives forever.

To Kill a Mockingbird
H. Lee
Warner Books

A story of life in a small Southern town from the eyes of a young girl, Scout. The reader learns what it means to stand up to prejudice and injustice.

Watership Down
R. Adams
Avon Books

A hardy band of adventurers are forced to flee the destruction of their fragile community and pursue a glorious dream called "home."

Shared Reading Time Activities

Make reading a fun, meaningful part of your interactions with your child. You can accomplish this in many ways as simple or elaborate as your schedule permits. Choose the ideas below that best suit your child's grade level and interests. Then begin by setting aside 30 minutes each day to read. Include time reading aloud to each other, and also time reading silently, side by side. Imagine the number of volumes you can cover by the time your child leaves home if you spend a half hour a day together. Use these activities to enhance your reading experience.

Elementary School

Make a book cover.
Ask your child to draw and color an original design for a cover for a book you've read together.

Share an experience.
Write or tell about an experience you've had that was similar to an experience of a story character.

Make stick puppets.
Younger children may want to draw, color and cut out story characters from a book they have read. Attach each character to a craft stick or straw. Reread favorite story parts using the puppets as performers. Put on a performance for the whole family.

Middle School and High School

Share the news.
Create a shared reading time in your schedule each day. If this is not possible, at least choose to read one evening every week when your child does not have extra-curricular activities. Acquaint your child with the various sections of the newspaper. Read an article together or separately each day and discuss it. (Mealtime is a good time for discussion.) Give your child a fluorescent pen to highlight any unfamiliar words, and look them up together in the dictionary.

Stage a family drama.
Take a trip to your local library and check out the 810 and 812 book stacks. You'll find hundreds of plays that make perfect oral reading activities. You may also find screenplays and movie scripts in the 791.437 section. Encourage the family to participate in a reader's theater. Even the non-readers in the family can participate by creating sound effects. You may want to recreate the reading at a family reunion or holiday gathering.

Comic Books
Many preteens and teens are captivated by the world of comic books. Share the comic-book experience together by reading the dialogue aloud—with feeling! Ask your child to read appropriate material to younger brothers and sisters. An appreciative audience is great motivation.

Give magazine subscriptions.
Consider giving a magazine subscription to your child as a birthday or holiday gift. Ask your child to share interesting articles from the magazine with the family. Today's magazines address many current trends of interest to the preteen and teen reader. For magazine ideas, check the local library.

Go Online.
You may want to send your child to the Internet to research locations for a family vacation or topics of interest to the whole family, or to expand the child's learning in some area. Electronic libraries make it possible to find reference descriptions and critiques of books and authors. Search engines direct users to information on virtually any topic, from past astronaut excursions to future family vacations. Sit with your child in the beginning and bookmark the sites you want to return to. You may also want to purchase CD-ROMs designed to enhance literacy or learning.

Web Resources for Working with Non-English-Speaking Parents

American Federation of Teachers (AFT)

555 New Jersey Avenue, NW
Washington, DC 20001
202-879-4400
www.aft.org

AFT helps teachers at state and local levels with collective bargaining, public relations and research. Areas of research include bilingual education. AFT-sponsored Learning Activities Hotline: 1-800-242-5465.

Involving Hispanic Parents in Their Children's Education

www.topher.net/~spurgeon/

Parents can play a significant role in helping their children succeed in American schools. This report includes suggested information for parents and constructive steps that educators can take.

Model Strategies in Bilingual Education

www.ncbe.gwu.edu/miscpubs/used/familylit

This report offers teachers and administrators examples of many strategies used to work with parents of students designated with Limited English Proficiency (LEP), profiling exemplary sites with a wide range of parent involvement and family literacy programs.

Parental Involvement (Los Padres Participan)

eric-web.tc.columbia.edu/abstracts /ed285400.html

This manual contains materials developed for Spanish-speaking parents in New York City's Community School District 3 that may be useful for other bilingual parent populations in need of English-language learning.

Translation Search

rivendel.com/~ric/resources/dictionary.html

When writing letters of introduction, homework policies and other standard parent communications, go to the Web for translation in the languages the parents speak. Some sites offer literal translations, so write the letter without idioms that might cause confusion. Try this site for free online translations in many languages.

Please Come to
Back-to-School Night!

Date: _____ Time: _____ Room: _____

To the parents of: _____

Here's your chance to:

- See what we're doing in class.

- Watch a special presentation starring your child.

- Learn what you can do at home to help your child succeed in school.

- See samples of your child's work.

- Take home a free parent handbook with information about our class curriculum, policies and more!

Baby-sitting will be available in Room 6.

- -

Please return this slip tomorrow.

☐ Yes, we will attend back-to-school night.
    We will bring _____ children who need child care.

☐ No, we cannot attend back-to-school night.

Signed: _____

You're Invited To
Back-to-School Night

Date: _____ Time: _____

Place: _____

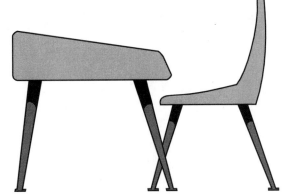

Follow this schedule so that you can meet your child's teachers and learn about the upcoming school year.

Period	Class	Teacher	Room #	Time
_____	_____	_____	_____	_____
_____	_____	_____	_____	_____
_____	_____	_____	_____	_____
_____	_____	_____	_____	_____
_____	_____	_____	_____	_____
_____	_____	_____	_____	_____
_____	_____	_____	_____	_____

This will be a very special night, so let's support our students!

Looking forward to seeing you.

Parent Conference Invitation

To the parents of: _____.

During the week of _____, I will be holding parent-teacher conferences. I look forward to talking with you about your child's education this year. We have an important job to do: to make this a productive, happy year for your child. At the conference we will discuss your child's progress, my goals for the year, and any other issues that affect your child. I am certain that by working together, we can make this the best year ever for your child.

I have scheduled your parent conference for

    Day: _____   Date: _____   Time: _____.

Please fill out the RSVP portion of this invitation and send it back to school. If you have any questions you'd like to discuss with me at the conference, please write them on the form. It's important that we have the opportunity to talk about issues that are important to you.

Sincerely,

_____

- -

RSVP

_____ Yes, I can attend the parent conference at the scheduled time.

_____ No, I can't make the scheduled time. If possible, please reschedule me for

    Day: _____   Date: _____   Time: _____.

I would like to discuss these concerns at the conference: _____

_____

_____

Parent's signature: _____   Student's name: _____

Confirmation

Dear Parent,

I have rescheduled your parent conference for

    Day: _____   Date: _____   Time: _____.

Please contact me if this is inconvenient.

Teacher's signature: _____

Parent Conference Planning Sheet

Use a copy of this sheet to prepare for your conference with each student's parents:

Parent's Name: _____   Conference Date: _____

Student's Name: _____   Time: _____

1. Example of student's unique quality: _____

    _____

2. Past problems to be updated at the conference: _____

    _____

3. Academic strengths of the student: _____

    _____

4. Academic weaknesses that should be discussed: _____

    _____

5. Academic goals for the student for the rest of the year: _____

    _____

6. Parent input on student's academic performance: _____

    _____

7. Social strengths of the student: _____

    _____

8. Weaknesses in the area of social development: _____

    _____

9. Social development goals for the rest of the year: _____

    _____

10. Parent input regarding student's social behavior: _____

    _____

11. Additional issues parent wishes to discuss: _____

    _____

Additional conference notes: _____

    _____

    _____

Open House Invitation

Instructions:

To make your own personalized invitation:

1. Cut along the line below these instructions.
2. Draw yourself inside the doorway.

- -

Please come to our Open House!

Time: _____ Date: _____ Room:_____

You will see lots of interesting things in our classroom.

Look inside the door to find one of them.

I Am Your Tour Guide

Created Especially for the _____ Family

By_____

Welcome to Room _____. I will lead you on an exciting tour to show you five of my favorite things in the classroom. Each time you see one, write your comments below, so our family can keep this as a keepsake of this school year. Enjoy the tour.

My five favorites: **Please write your comments here:**

1. _____

I enjoyed seeing this because:

2. _____

I can see why you like this, because:

3. _____

Wow! This item shows me that:

4. _____

I'm glad you shared this with me. It's important because:

5. _____

Good choice. I like this because:

CHAPTER 4

How to Engage Students in Learning

4

" Teaching means being so
planned and so regimented on
paper, but when it comes to the
class, the paper doesn't matter.
It's a living, breathing moment.
When I get the kids excited
about learning, I think, 'I'm
really doing this—I'm teaching!' "

Do you recall the teacher you envisioned when you decided to become a teacher? Did you have a special role model—a teacher who aroused your motivation to learn? Many people can pick a favorite but cannot quite identify what made the teacher so effective in expanding their world.

What does it take to truly engage students in learning? A belief in the students' ability? Enthusiasm about the subject matter? The skills to dynamically communicate the content? Creative lesson plans? The ability to make students think as well as have fun? A commitment to reaching out to every student?

Yes, it takes all of the above.

In this chapter, you will find helpful tools and strategies to help you develop that magic combination of qualities that will make you "somebody's hero" and, perhaps, an inspiration to *tomorrow's* teachers.

"Sell" the Day

One of the most powerful services a teacher can deliver is to help students anticipate each day as an exciting learning opportunity. Your enthusiasm can teach them to see knowledge as a gift that they open with pleasure.

Generate curiosity about your daily lesson plans and help students visualize the accomplishments they can expect to achieve. The strategies that follow will let you turn anticipation into a habit.

- Begin each day on a positive note. Provide a regular morning activity (or an activity at the beginning of the period) that sets an upbeat "I can do it" tone right from the start. See page 31 in Chapter 1 for ideas.

- In the morning, distribute the "Why It's Going to Be a Great Day" worksheet provided in the resource section at the end of this chapter. As you describe the day's agenda, ask students to write down one topic they look forward to learning about and one new skill they want to work on today. If your students do not write yet, pair them and have them tell each other what they anticipate.

- At the end of the day, distribute the "Why It Was a Great Day" worksheet in the resource section. Have your students take two to three minutes to write down, draw or tell something they learned or did well. Have students take these reflections home and share them with their parents.

- For older students, begin each class period by writing movie ad "teaser" phrases on the board to create enthusiasm: "Measuring an Isosceles Triangle—a classic! Will be remembered for generations to come! Not to be missed! — Mr. Lederer, esteemed critic for the Geometry Daily News."

Why It's Going to Be a Great Day
Page 151

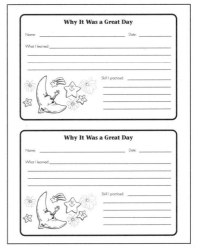

Why It Was a Great Day
Page 152

4

Polish Your Presentation Skills

You can help students look forward to learning by sharing your own contagious enthusiasm. Start by evaluating your presentation skills. Think about your own favorite teacher, storyteller, actor or public speaker. Does this person look you straight in the eye while talking, or make expressive gestures, or use varying tones of voice to convey meaning or emotion? Does this person seem to speak to you personally?

Your job as a teacher pivots around the task of doing just that—passing on a personal sense of wonderment about your content. As you identify the skills you would look for in a dynamic presentation and begin using them, you will find it easier to engage students in learning and welcome them to a new field of discovery.

Rehearse a lesson you plan to teach, incorporating the following presentation strategies until you feel comfortable with them.

Tip 1: Use Emotive Facial Expressions. Convey your excitement about the topic and keep your students' attention by using your face to exude warmth, humor or drama.

Tip 2: Make Eye Contact. As you complete a thought, look at one student and hold eye contact slightly longer than he or she is accustomed to. This student will receive your message more clearly, and other students will also pay attention.

Tip 3: Incorporate Body Movements. Your body can become your best visual aid. Energize your presentation by using gesturing to convey meaning or emotion and by acting animated. Feel free to move around the room to demonstrate action or to draw every student into a story or presentation.

Tip 4: Vary Your Tone of Voice. Listen to yourself as you talk to others. Note the relationship between your tone of voice and their reactions. Experiment with various pitches and volumes. An interesting voice keeps students listening and paying attention to what you say.

Learn Involvement Strategies

Video games . . . interactive computer games . . . television . . . movies. Your greatest competition for your students' attention may come from outside the classroom walls. Today's students, no matter how bright, tend to come to school with greater "entertainment" expectations than students of past generations. As a new teacher, how can you compete with all the other excitement in a student's life?

The answer lies in maximizing student involvement. When students play the role of "participants" instead of "audience members," your classroom can become as exciting as the local arcade. Of course, in the classroom, interactivity does not usually mean asking students to push buttons or steer joy sticks. It means challenging students to use their minds. It means presenting ideas that kindle the imagination, engage the senses or fulfill the human search for meaning.

Apply the involvement strategies in this section to tap your students' potential and to keep them feeling involved and motivated. Preview the tips listed and choose a few to try out in class. When you feel comfortable with one strategy, try another. Before long, these techniques will become a natural part of your teaching repertoire.

Spotlight Every Student

Children tend to want to live up to their parents' and teachers' expectations, and their self-perceptions may develop based on your belief in them. Show that you believe in all your students by calling on and listening to each one.

Research tells us that teachers often unconsciously maintain lower academic expectations for some students based on issues such as prior achievement, gender or race. Remember, the equity with which you set your expectations lets students know that you trust them to make their best effort.

Students often expect to disengage early in a class discussion. For instance, have you ever noticed the facial expressions of students after a teacher asks a question? As soon as a hand goes up and a teacher praises the "right answer," the other faces go slack. Students seldom called upon sometimes become bored and stop thinking about the content. By giving each student a voice in class, you can ensure that each one stays interested in the discussion and also senses your high expectations for their learning.

Strive to help all your students feel comfortable and valued. Help them see themselves as contributors. Take the following steps to see how well you give every student a chance to think and participate.

- Make a list of the students who seem to participate the most. Make another list of those who participate the least.

- Conduct a self-analysis. Ask yourself whether you respond differently to the students on these two lists. Ask: Do I call on some students more than others? Do I ever ignore some students or let them just get by because I expect too little of them? Do I call on certain students as a means of managing their behavior? Do I forget to involve the quiet, shy students?

- You may want to have an aide keep track of the number of times you call on each student during one day, or have the aide videotape your interactions with students. Observe the reactions of those who do not get much of your attention.

- Jot down the names of a few students whom you will try to encourage to participate more often. Hold casual conversations that express your interest and support.

Read through the strategies on the next page and identify ways you might engage all students. Check off each strategy as you use it. Decide which ones work best for your students and use them frequently.

4

Involvement Strategies: Calling on All Students

☐ Use Wait Time

Research shows that students tend to tune out once the teacher calls on someone who knows "the right answer." Resist the tendency to call on the first hands raised. Wait for many students to raise their hands before calling on anyone. Tell students that you're going to wait so they will continue to raise their hands even after the first few students do so. Count slowly to five or six before calling on a student.

Wait time refers not only to waiting before you call on a student but also to pausing after a student has spoken. Instead of quickly moving on to get the answer you want, listen carefully and give students a chance to think about each response. Call on several students before you comment.

☐ Pass the Baton

Encourage each student to participate by asking a question with a range of possible responses. Next, have students sit in a circle and pass around a soft ball, stuffed animal or other object. As students pass the object around, each one adds something to the answers already given, so they layer their responses rather than stopping with one easy answer or letting one student dominate the discussion.

For instance, if you ask, "What did the character in the story feel?" one student might say, "Lonely." The next might add, "Angry at his father." The next student might say, "Afraid to ask for help."

☐ Pull Names from a Hat

When asking a question of the entire class, use some techniques that do not involve hand raising. Pull several names out of a hat and have those students answer, or point to a name on the class list or in the roll book to make sure you call on students in a random fashion.

☐ Ask for a Signal

Give all students "think time." Ask them to signal when they have an answer by putting their hands on their shoulders or head, or by giving some other signal. When most students have signaled that they're ready, ask everyone to put their hands down. Because everyone has had a chance to think, you can call on any student in the room.

Reach Out to Reluctant Students

Many new teachers feel frustrated in their attempts to involve every student because some students do not feel inclined to respond verbally in class discussions. Shyness or language barriers sometimes inhibit their responses.

Rather than ignoring these nonverbal students in class, you can provide opportunities for them to respond without the embarrassment of speaking aloud in front of the group. Read through each of the following response strategies. In addition to helping nonverbal students, these techniques can add variety to your instruction strategies.

Involvement Strategies:
Give Nonverbal Students a Voice

☐ **Allow Silent Signals**

Pose a question, thought or problem and ask students to respond in a nonverbal way, such as raising their hands, showing thumbs up to agree with a statement or thumbs down to disagree, writing answers on individual slates, or holding up word or number cards.

☐ **Ask for a Choral Response**

Help students internalize or memorize material by responding to a question aloud, in unison. You can use this technique with flash cards or other teacher prompts. For instance, hold up a math flash card and have students give the answer in unison. This strategy works especially well for students who feel uncomfortable when singled out.

☐ **Call for a Vote**

Ask questions students can respond to nonverbally at will, such as: "How many of you... ?" The question may relate to students' prior knowledge of the new information you will present. (Examples: "How many of you have thrown a stone into a lake or river and watched ripples form in the water? How many of you feel you understand the 'ripple' effect? How many of you would like to discuss a few more examples?") Students may nod or raise their hand in response to these questions, making it easy for them to participate and for you to sample student thinking without slowing the pace of the lesson.

☐ **Let Students Record Responses**

Present material to the class, periodically giving students time to write a response, such as a personal reaction, a summary of what they heard, or a question that occurs to them. For instance, when giving an oral presentation, stop and ask students to summarize the key points. This strategy offers students an opportunity to think about, synthesize and retain ideas even if they do not share their ideas in class.

☐ **Let Each Student Share with a Partner**

Students who do not feel comfortable speaking out in a large group may feel more willing to talk with another student. As a follow-up to the last strategy, let each student share his or her written response with a partner before you call on volunteers to verbalize their answers for the entire class.

☐ **Encourage Collaboration**

Take the sharing process one step further by having students present the content to each other rather than asking them to respond to you. Form small groups and have students read aloud and discuss the content within their groups.

4

Make the Most of Questions

Asking questions allows teachers to immediately draw students into full participation. It lets students see the search for knowledge as a shared experience. It enhances learning by challenging students to analyze, sort and assimilate information. It increases retention through personal discovery. You can use questions to:

- Pique students' interest about a new topic.

- Expand students' critical thinking about a subject.

- Review material.

- Assess student learning.

Vary the ways in which you use questions to keep students engaged. Try the questioning strategies that follow.

Involvement Strategies:
Cue Them with Questions

☐ Start a Question Chain

Ask a question and give the answer. (Example: "What is the formula for finding the area of a triangle?" "The area of a triangle equals one half the base times the height.") Then turn to a student and ask the same question. That student responds with the answer and then turns to another student and poses the same question. The students repeat the cycle until each one has participated. This strategy offers a highly involving method for students to internalize a fact or review subject matter that you want them to memorize.

☐ Send Questions Down the Line

Pose a question with several possible responses, such as "Can you list some of the characteristics of mammals?" Convey that you believe each student might have a unique response to the question. Ask each student to either add a piece of information or say, "I pass. Please come back to me when I've had a chance to hear other answers."

☐ Promote Higher Level Questioning

Scaffolding your questions can stimulate critical thinking and engage each type of learner. To "scaffold" means to ask questions that lead students from recalling basic facts to explaining to speculating. Moving from first-level to second- and third-level questions can help students more fully understand the lesson content. Use this guide as a reference. The examples show how you might scaffold your questions during a discussion of the first moon landing.

- **First-level questions** require fact collection—counting, defining, describing, listing, naming, or recalling data. Use verbal cues such as "who," "what," "where," and "when."

  Example: Who participated in the first moon landing? When did it occur?

- **Second-level questions** involve the processing of information—comparing, contrasting, classifying, distinguishing or explaining. Pose the questions "how" and "why."

  Example: How did the astronauts conduct their research? Why did they go to the moon?

- **Third-level questions** encourage students to see relationships and patterns—evaluating, hypothesizing, imagining, predicting or idealizing. Ask "what if" questions that require speculative thinking.

  Example: What if they had discovered mammals living on the moon? What if they had brought earthly mammals to live on the moon? What would have happened to the astronauts if they stayed to live on the moon for an extended period of time?

☐ **Set the Stage with a Question**

Prime students' curiosity at the beginning of a chapter or unit by asking an open-ended question such as one of the following:

- What can you tell me about _____?
- How do you explain _____?
- What would you like to invent, knowing what you know about _____?

Bring the Content to Life

First-class teachers—teachers who truly engage students in learning—go a step beyond polishing their presentation style and refining their involvement strategies. They bring a creative flair to their curriculum. Your personal touches, in fact, may determine how well your students absorb and apply the lessons you teach, and how well they meet the broader educational standards set for them. There are several ways to bring your content to life: by gearing your instruction to your students' needs and capacities, by emphasizing the relevance and practicality of the learning in students' lives, and by creatively using the tools available to you.

Gear Instruction to Students' Unique Learning Needs

Every student comes into the classroom with a different personality, family culture and set of life experiences. It should not surprise teachers that each one also comes with a different learning orientation. Some students enjoy drills and memorization. Others learn best from discussion and verbal tasks. Others feel most comfortable creating things, working with their hands or relating to music. Many students today are adept at using a computer for such tasks as word processing and using the Internet to gather information. Bringing the content to life means allowing students to spend some time learning in the way they learn best, and some time developing new skills.

Resist the urge to teach only the way you were taught or to present the types of lessons you would enjoy as a student. Instead, try to add enough variety to your assignments that you appeal to each student's strengths sometimes and help them develop new strengths at other times. Honor each student's unique style of learning by continually looking for new approaches that will meet the needs of every student over the course of the day or week.

Use the "Understanding Your Students" listing in the resource section to ensure that you create learning experiences that address the needs and ability levels of all students. Taking a course on learning styles or multiple intelligences may help you broaden your understanding of individual differences.

Reproduce the "Checklist for Varying Your Instruction" in the resource section to make sure your lesson plans engage every learner.

Lend Relevance to Learning

Relevance amplifies learning. Brain research shows that when students see ways to apply new knowledge, they can better retain that knowledge. When they learn within the context of their own experience, they can store and retrieve the information more readily.

Look at your learning objectives and preview the content you need to cover, then determine how to help students find meaning in the learning. Show them the significance of the content to their own lives. For instance, a teacher trying to convey the social impact of the Civil War can add relevance to the content in many ways, at various points in the learning process. Each of the ideas on the facing page, "Civil War Learning Strategies," might help students sense the significance of the Civil War. Each strategy includes an element to help students relate the information to their experience or time period.

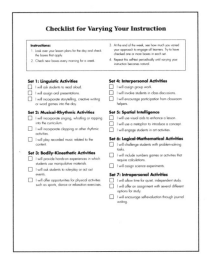

Understanding Your Students
Page 153–154

Checklist for Varying Your Instruction
Page 155

Civil War Learning Strategies

Introductory Strategy: Bring Them to the Scene

Teacher: "How many of you have a cousin who lives in another state? Call out which state. (*Point out the states on the map.*) What would you do if our state went to war with the state where your cousin lives? You already feel devastated at the thought of hurting others in hand-to-hand combat. How would you feel if you suddenly faced your cousin, fighting for the other side?

"The Civil War put people in that same position. It pitted neighboring states against one another. It disrupted families. At the same time, it helped many people gain the freedom to return to their family members because the Civil War led to the freeing of the slaves. You can imagine how confusing it must have felt to live in those times."

Presentation Strategy: Wear a Visual Aid

Teacher: "Look at this cotton T-shirt I brought in today. Think of all the cotton clothing you wear. When the Southern plantation owners gained access to the cotton gin, they sent for more slaves and grew a great deal of cotton through the use of slave labor. Cotton sustained their economy. They felt threatened by the thought of losing their plantations and not being able to grow cotton any more. These concerns probably made it harder for them to look objectively at the social impact of the war and at the social impact of slavery. We will discuss some of the reasons the Southerners made the choices they did."

Discussion Strategy: Assess the Impact

Teacher: "How did the war change the way people lived and related to one another? What would have happened if the South had won the war? How would this have influenced the lives of the people living at that time? How might it have influenced the lives of Americans living today? "

Activity Strategy: Conduct Relevant Role-Plays

Teacher: "Students, let's conduct a role-play. Meet with your partner. One of you will act as Ulysses S. Grant. The other will play the role of Robert E. Lee. Each one of you must explain to the other the impact of the war upon your people and try to persuade your opponent to become sympathetic to your side. When you have finished, we will meet and list the points you made in your role-plays."

Follow-up Strategy: Find Real-World Parallels

Teacher: "Interview people you know who witnessed or participated in a war. Ask how it changed them. Ask how they felt after the war. Now write two journal entries dated just after the Civil War—one as if you had been a soldier for the Confederate army and one as if you were a freed female slave. Describe your life circumstances and your feelings about the war. How do they relate to the feelings of the modern-day war survivors you interviewed?"

4

Suggest Practical Applications for Learning

Students generally feel more excited about learning information they can use in their everyday lives. Whatever your curriculum or grade level, you can help students find practical applications for their learning. A lesson in geometry can become a birdhouse that students construct. A science experiment can become a recipe they take home. A Language Arts exercise in writing poetry can become a Mother's Day gift.

Offer tools that help students focus on applying the knowledge they attain. The "Learning Bank" student worksheet provided in the resource section lets students review, apply and record their learning. If you use it, you may want to compile the completed sheets in your students' portfolios.

Learning Bank
Page 156

See the examples on the facing page to imagine how you might adapt the skills bank for your students. Before you offer the worksheet, remember to explain the concept of making deposits at a bank. Explain that adults put money in a bank account as they work and receive paychecks. Later in the month, when they need to purchase something, they can use the money in their bank account. Describe how a brain works similarly. The knowledge you deposit now comes in handy later when you need to use it for practical purposes.

4

Learning Bank

Example for Math

Deposits	Dividends
(What I learned)	(How I drew new skills from my learning and used them in my life)
I learned long division.	I used my knowledge to find out how many baseball-card packs I could buy with a month's allowance.

Learning Bank

Example for Science

Deposits	Dividends
(What I learned)	(How I drew new skills from my learning and used them in my life)
I learned how pulleys work.	I drew on my learning to help my brother fix his bike.

Learning Bank

Example for Spanish

Deposits	Dividends
(What I learned)	(How I drew new skills from my learning and used them in my life)
I learned how to say "hello," "please," "thank you," "How are you?" and "I'm fine."	I made friends with a lady who lives in my apartment building, who speaks only Spanish. I say a few words to her every day. She gives me flowers from her garden and I say "gracias."

4

Carefully Choose Your Tools

Teachers once relied on chalkboards and chalk to get through the day. Today's first-class teachers use an increasingly greater range of tools to help them facilitate learning and engage students. The hands-on approach to learning means giving students opportunities to collect, discuss, organize and share the information. It means introducing them to the tools many will use in their life's work, such as computers, telephones and even video cameras.

Your creative use of technological tools and teaching aids can not only support your learning goals but bring the content to life. However, resources are not always distributed equitably from school to school and from district to district. If budgetary constraints limit your teaching tools, you may want to add some materials—such as art supplies, electronic equipment and books—by visiting yard sales and mentioning your needs to friends. You may be surprised at how much you can collect just by asking.

The increasing range of learning tools available reflects the reality students will inherit as they enter the workplace. Regardless of their specialty, employers will probably expect their employees to know how to use the right tools for the job. When you introduce a new learning tool, make sure the usage supports your goals for learning and also lends relevance to the experience. Consider the following suggestions:

- Use a class camera to document the growth of a plant or animal in science class.
- Use a video camera to tape a class play about your town's history. Offer the tape to the local library or historical society as a resource.
- Use donated materials to have students construct a useful object used in the time period they have studied. For instance, if students are reading *The Patchwork Quilt*, (see page 115), have them bring in scraps of fabric and make a class quilt.
- Use a tape recorder to show students their growth over time as new readers.
- Assign projects requiring the computer for research or presentation and have students share the presentation with a real audience.

The computer has perhaps more potential to revolutionize learning than any of the other new tools available. While some schools struggle to provide basic supplies, others have enriched their resources through technology grants. An increasing number of school districts have already wired their classrooms to the Internet.

New teachers often have an advantage over veteran teachers when using Internet technology. Your recent experience in a university or in the workplace may have given you more expertise in computer technologies than some of the other teachers in your school. On the other hand, a few of your students may know as much or more than you do about the technology. Your vision of how to use the tools to teach your specific content is really more crucial than the level of your technical expertise. Review these tips if you decide to assign work on the Internet.

4

Technology Tips

- Assign projects that encourage students to ask relevant questions about the content. For instance, a science lesson on oxygen might lead students to ask about the impact of air pollution and to conduct an Internet poll about air quality in various cities.

- Make sure your assignments teach students new research skills while honoring traditional skills. For instance, an assignment might challenge students to find historical photos to support the textual information they read, by contacting the Library of Congress online. Or the assignment might require that they go to the Internet to look up directories of books or information they will obtain at the library.

- Teach collaboration through online group work. The groups may consist of team members each assigned to do a portion of the research, or it may extend to student-groups from other schools who collaborate online to compile information.

- Think of projects that connect students to a broader community. As students contact agencies and individuals outside the school, they may begin to sense the relevance of their work. For instance, one class developed online pen pals in a retirement home who helped them study an earlier period in American history.

- Consider assignments that offer a real-world experience or that help students create a useful product. Some classes have created their own Web sites with a museum of their town. In other schools individual students create Web pages or CD-ROMs. Still others communicate with outside agencies online to provide information such as weather observations, water quality testing, or wildlife counts. These classes play a valuable role as contributors to society.

- While you are new as a teacher, you may prefer to tap into existing Internet projects rather than creating your own. Explore the classroom resources and partnership projects on the "Web Project Resource Sites" list in the resource section.

Web Project Resource Sites
Pages 157–158

Promote Learning with Fun Fillers

Once you have engaged students with sparkling presentations, thoughtful involvement strategies and meaningful learning activities, you may begin to feel like a first-class teacher. Take it one step further and plan activities for those unexpected extra moments. Keep a potpourri of quick learning activities at your fingertips for occasions when you finish a lesson early or when your schedule suddenly changes. For instance, if your class has already lined up to go to an assembly when you learn that the assembly has been delayed ten minutes, use the time to stimulate students' minds. Try the following ideas:

Assign Impromptu Activities

- List as many nouns as you can see.

- Draw your favorite animal. Tell what you know about the animal.

- Make a list of your five favorite books and share them with a partner.

- Write word problems to go with this math problem: 24 + 31. (Vary the problem according to what students are studying.)

- List as many continents (countries, states, cities in our state) as you can.

- Practice: spelling words, math facts, etc.

Pose Puzzles and Riddles

- Run off copies of several crossword puzzles or other puzzles to hand out.

- Put math puzzlers or logic games on the board. (Good sources include math books, brain-teaser books and teacher magazines.)

- Fill a minute or two by having a student pull a riddle out of a box and quiz the class. Cut out and use the "Classroom Cut-Ups" reproducible in the resource section.

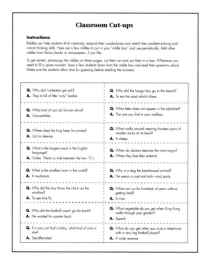

Classroom Cut-ups
Page 159-161

Conduct Class Games

An occasional class game can enliven the daily routine and can also fill time between activities. Teacher publications often offer game ideas. Try these games:

- **Buzz**

  Go around the room, having each student say the next number as they count to 100. But each time a multiple of three comes up, the student says "buzz" instead of the number. (Vary the game by using multiples of other numbers. To make it more exciting, try speeding up the game.)

4

- **Guess What I'm Doing**

  Think of a math operation such as "times 4," but don't tell students. Have them take turns giving you numbers. Your response is their number multiplied by 4. (A student says "3" so you answer "12.") If a student thinks he or she has guessed the operation, test the student by giving two or three additional numbers. The student who guesses correctly gets to think of the next operation and quiz the class.

- **I Spy**

  Use a variation of this game by giving clues that include vocabulary or concepts you've been studying. For example, clues might include: "I spy something that starts with a b." "It is symmetrical." "It has horizontal lines."

Assess for Success

Some people think of assessment as something that happens after the learning process has ended—in other words, when you give a test. Yet, in fact, the assessment tools you choose and the timing with which you use them can help you engage your students and enhance their learning, especially if you observe these guidelines:

- Choose some assessment strategies that encourage students to master skills and improve their performance.

- Assess student work when students are still thinking about the particular skill or project and still have time to make those improvements rather than waiting until the end of a semester. This allows you to evaluate the effectiveness of your own teaching strategies and understand what content areas need more explanation or review.

- Sometimes, let them assess their own work or discuss the class definition of quality work. The more students feel involved in the assessment of their work, the more they will feel motivated to improve.

Give Prompt Feedback

First-year teachers often face an adjustment period as they learn to juggle time spent preparing assignments and time spent assessing them. As a result, students may study the material and take the test but forget the subject matter by the time the teacher distributes the corrected exams. Or they may work hard on a project and the year ends before they receive any teacher feedback. Students benefit most from feedback received when the assignment is still fresh in their minds. Take the following safeguards to ensure promptness:

- Prioritize. Let students grade each other's quizzes or worksheets while you save your time for the assessments that require a more subjective analysis, such as essays, projects and exams.

- Assign the deadlines for major projects realistically. For instance, if you know you have to drive all weekend to attend a friend's out-of-state wedding, don't assume you will find time to grade 100 essay exams by the time you return on Monday. Give the papers an earlier or later deadline, so you can assess them promptly after students turn them in.

- When you plan your weekly schedule, allow as much time—or more—for evaluating student work as you allow for planning. Allow time to make constructive comments on each paper.

Carefully Choose Assessment Tools

Make sure you put as much thought into your assessments as you put in your assignments. Match the assessment tool with your specific learning objectives. For instance:

- Assess basic knowledge through quizzes and tests using multiple choice, fill-in and true or false questions.

- Assess a student's ability to synthesize and expand on the learning through carefully conceived essay questions.

- Assess students' ability to apply their learning through performances and student-created products.

- Assess students' growth over time using portfolios that include work samples reflecting students' knowledge, skills and understanding.

- Assess students' level of mastery in a specific area with rubrics.

These are just a few of the assessment tools in use in today's classrooms. Ask the evaluation specialists in your district for more ideas.

Plan for Effective Tests

We've all taken tests for so many years that you would think creating one would be easy, but there's a certain art to creating an effective test.

Remember that the primary purpose of testing is not to rank students but to evaluate the depth of their learning. Try using Bloom's Taxonomy as a guide when designing a teacher-created test. Educational theorist Benjamin Bloom identified progressive levels of cognitive ability. You can use certain words or questions to trigger each of these levels of cognition. Use the reference sheet "Create a Test Using Bloom's Taxonomy" as a guide to create a test on the "Test-Maker's Worksheet." These worksheets will help you adapt Bloom's Taxonomy to evaluate the depth of your students' understanding of the content. Both worksheets are provided in the resource section. Keep a supply on hand to use whenever you create a test for your students.

Create a Test Using Bloom's Taxonomy
Page 162–163

How you write a test is important, but when you give it and how much emphasis you place on it can also influence students' learning and performance. Consider the following strategies when you sit down to plan your tests.

Give Mini-tests

Frequent small tests offer some benefits over fewer large ones. They provide continual feedback to the teacher regarding the efficacy of your instruction and to the student regarding the potency of the learning. They minimize test anxiety and offer students a chance for several small successes. They reveal problems more quickly.

Test-Maker's Worksheet
Page 164

Involve Students

Students can test each other orally in fact-based subjects such as spelling or math. For content areas involving essay questions, let students write sample questions in advance. Involving students can make the testing process more fun and less threatening.

For example, you might suggest, "I would like each of you to write three essay questions that you could answer based on what we've learned in this unit. Then write a one-paragraph answer. Some of you may choose the same questions, but that's all right because your answers will vary. Your questions will help me see what we need to review. I may include some of your questions on the final test."

Give Check-ups

Between tests, use frequent reviews to see how well students are internalizing the material. Include in your review some questions that challenge students to apply the learning in new contexts.

Encourage Self-Mastery with Rubrics

Some teachers find it helpful to develop rubrics to assess major projects. A rubric is a grid-shaped scoring tool that shows progressive levels of mastery and includes descriptions of those levels. A sophisticated learning tool, the rubric helps both students and teachers identify the *criteria* for assessing performance. A rubric works best with students old enough to read and understand it. You may prefer simpler assessment methods for early elementary students.

Rubrics provide several benefits. Students can refer to a rubric frequently to check the quality of their work. Teachers can use the rubric to grade the completed work. A rubric may take some time to develop, but the effort it takes to create an effective rubric can pay off when parents question students' grades. You can confidently show the criteria you used to determine the grade and explain your standards for quality work to the parent.

When designing a rubric, identify areas and levels of mastery you want students to achieve. Describe in detail what the work looks like when performed at each level and help students set goals that lean toward that higher level.

In the example on the facing page, an eighth-grade literature teacher uses a writing assignment to measure student learning after completing a unit on "Authors Who Create a Sense of Place." Students each research an author's era and write a narrative passage about a place where the author might have set a story. This assignment lets students *apply* rather than just *report* their learning. The rubric guides their efforts and makes it easier for you to assess the work. As you review the example, think about the possible criteria for developing a rubric based on your curriculum.

Notice that this rubric does not rate students by letter grade or point value, yet it has four levels of mastery, which the teacher could later convert to letter grades. In the example shown, a student who turns in a "classic" paper in every category would earn an A+. The other levels would translate to A, B, and C.

Rubric Example
Narrative Writing: A Sense of Place

Aspects of Performance	Levels of Mastery			
	Shows Potential	**A Good Read**	**A Best-Seller**	**A Classic**
Imagery	Elements of the setting are mentioned but not described.	Descriptions of the place give some detail about the appearance of the place but the reader must imagine the rest.	Descriptions of the setting give enough detail to help the reader truly visualize the place.	Descriptions of the setting evoke all or most of the senses with sights, sounds, scents, tastes and feelings.
Metaphor and Simile	The passage does not make use of metaphor or simile in its descriptions.	The passage uses metaphor or simile but the examples given are forced or do not contribute to the reader's understanding.	The passage uses either metaphor or simile effectively; usage makes unfamiliar objects, feelings or ideas more "real" to the reader.	The passage uses both metaphor and simile; usage makes unfamiliar objects, feelings or ideas more "real" to the reader.
Research Basis for Setting	The passage includes at least one specific reference to the landscape, architecture, clothing, customs or people of the period.	The passage includes at least two specific references to the landscape, architecture, clothing, customs or people of the period.	The passage shows an in-depth understanding of either the landscape, architecture, culture, customs or people of the period.	The passage shows an in-depth understanding of the landscape, architecture, clothing, customs and people of the period.

4

As the example shows, project rubrics can help you assign letter grades if you need to, while recognizing developmental progress rather than mere success or failure.

To develop your own rubrics, reproduce the "Rubric" template provided in the resource section. Fill out one rubric for each major project and reproduce the finished rubric for your students. To fill out the rubric:

- Write the project name at the top.

- In the left column, list the aspects of performance you plan to assess.

- Label the levels of mastery at the top of each column.

- Fill in the criteria or descriptors for each area of assessment.

Rubric
Page 165

Design Your Grading System

As students approach middle school, grading becomes an increasingly emphasized aspect of education. Parents whose children received good grades in elementary school may question you about why their children suddenly did not perform well in a subject. You will need to explain the range of criteria you use to assess student work and how you broke out the grading scale. For instance, a student may not perform well on paper-and-pencil tests but may articulately participate in discussions or give effective oral presentations or display problem-solving skills. Likewise, a student who turns in all his or her homework may not show that he or she has assimilated the learning when asked to write or draw examples of the concept. Resist the tendency to reduce each student to a letter grade without considering and explaining the learning objectives and the levels of mastery the student achieved in each area.

Develop your grading system at the beginning of the year, so you can explain it to parents in your early correspondence. You can use a computerized grading system or see the example on the facing page for ideas. You may want to ask several colleagues what system has worked well for them, but do not be surprised if you receive conflicting advice. Choose a plan you feel comfortable with and stick with it. At the end of the year, you can evaluate how well your students and parents responded to see whether you need to make modifications.

Assessment Tip:
Sample Grading Scale

Teachers find many ways to assess student work. Most schools require that you translate those assessments into letter grades at the end of a grading period. Oral presentations, portfolios of student work, written assignments, tests and quizzes, and lab work or group projects often factor into a student's overall grade. Make students aware of your emphasis by presenting them with a scale such as the following:

Sample World Geography Grading Scale

Tests and Quizzes	20%
Homework	30%
– Completed and brought to class	
– Parent signature on calendar	
Classwork/Activities/Discussions	30%
Projects/Performances	20%
– Current events notebook	
– Historical role plays	
	_____
	100%

Sample Report Card Grading Scale

In middle school especially, many teachers assign points for each category and then average the numbers to compute the letter grade for the term or semester. If you use a numerical scoring system to arrive at a letter grade, first decide what assessment categories you will factor into the grade. Assign a point value to each category, based on a 100-point system. Use the example below to conceptualize how the percentages might translate into grades.

98–100 = A+	88–89 = B+	78–79 = C+	68–69 = D+
93–97 = A	83–87 = B	73–77 = C	63–67 = D
90–92 = A–	80–82 = B–	70–72 = C–	60–62 = D–
			50–59 = F

Note that if a student scores below 50%, you need to count the grade as a 50% score anyway. Otherwise, the low score will throw off the average and result in a lower letter grade than the student deserves. For example, if a student scored a 20%, a 92% and another 92%, the average percentage would be 68%, a D. Obviously, a student who earned an A on two thirds of the work should not receive a D. By counting the 25 as a 50, you raise the average to a more equitable 76%, so the final grade you assign is a C. Feel free to use a calculator and do not hesitate to refigure scores that don't look right to you.

Help Students Reflect on Their Learning

Students experience a major transition at the end of each year. They often must change teachers, enter a new grade level and sometimes even change schools. You can help them gain a sense of closure about their wonderful year in your classroom and also help them feel confident that they will adapt to the changes ahead. Try the following ideas:

Create a Keepsake

Have each student write a short essay about what they learned in your classroom. Compile a booklet of the written pieces. Add student art work or photos. If possible, make a copy of the booklet for each student to take home. In a class discussion, help students anticipate what they might learn next year.

Give a Sneak Preview

Invite a teacher from the next grade level to visit your classroom. Ask the guest teacher to discuss the highlights the students can expect the following year and suggest some summer reading or activities that will help them become enthusiastic about their new subject matter.

Help Students Set Goals

After the guest teacher's visit, have students write down their goals for personal growth during the following year and indicate what they hope to learn. Add a personal, positive message of your own. Give the students envelopes to address to themselves. Mail these self-addressed letters when the new school year begins.

Pass Along Portfolios

Let each student leave at the end of the year with a portfolio of his or her best work. Arrange for next year's teacher to ask for these portfolios at the beginning of school to give students the sense that they will carry their learning into the new year.

Give Send-off Assignments

Challenge your students to complete activities over the summer that will help them retain what they have learned throughout the year. Make a packet of fun activities, readings, suggested books and ideas for family "field trips." You will find reproducibles in Chapter 3, "How to Involve Parents." Include a piece of stationery, so students can write and let you know what activities they completed and what new information they learned over the summer. This gesture will help students value lifelong learning and feel more secure about their transition back to school. It will also let them know that your concern for their learning does not end with the close of the school year.

4

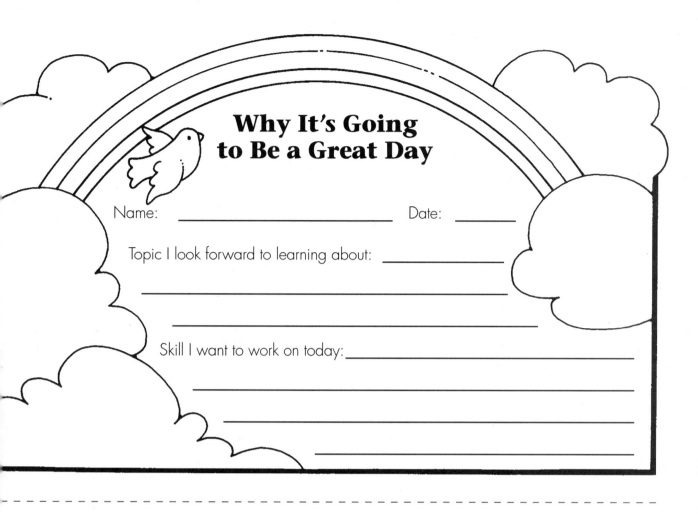

Why It's Going to Be a Great Day

Name: _____ Date: _____

Topic I look forward to learning about: _____

_____

_____

Skill I want to work on today: _____

_____

_____

_____

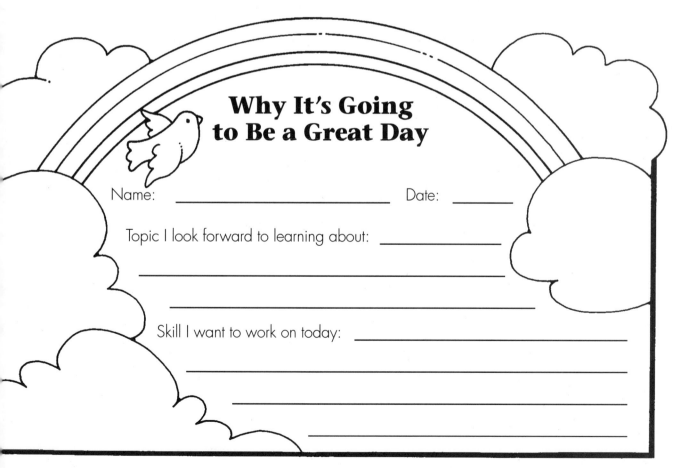

Why It's Going to Be a Great Day

Name: _____ Date: _____

Topic I look forward to learning about: _____

_____

_____

Skill I want to work on today: _____

_____

_____

_____

Why It Was a Great Day

Name: _____   Date: _____

What I learned: _____

_____

_____

_____

Skill I practiced: _____

_____

_____

_____

_____

Why It Was a Great Day

Name: _____   Date: _____

What I learned: _____

_____

_____

_____

Skill I practiced: _____

_____

_____

_____

_____

Understanding Your Students

Every student comes into the classroom with a unique personality, family background and level of cognitive, physical, emotional and moral development. However, students tend to exhibit different abilities and inclinations at each general stage of development.

Use this list of general tendencies to make your instruction, activities and interactions appropriate to your grade level, and to better understand your students' behavior and performance. You may also use it to understand which attributes are typical of a students' developmental level at a given age and which reflect unique learning traits.

Characteristics of Kindergartners

- Cheerfulness, high energy, enthusiasm
- Enjoy planning
- Enjoy dramatic play with other children
- Can skip, throw a ball and catch a bounced ball
- Use 5–8 words in a sentence
- Like to reason and explain
- Can memorize address and phone number
- Enjoy hearing and telling stories
- Can count up to 10
- Understand comparative terms
- Enjoy drawing
- Identify letters of the alphabet, if taught
- Understand categories
- Think in terms of projects
- Understand time concepts like yesterday, today and tomorrow
- May copy simple designs and shapes
- Invent games
- Still confuse fantasy with reality
- Like to try new things
- Notice when others are angry or sad

- Prefer working in groups of three or less
- Develop basic understanding of right and wrong
- Can work independently without constant supervision
- Enjoy giving and receiving
- Understand rules
- Need alone time
- Understand similarities and differences in other families
- Embarrassed by mistakes
- Develop sense of humor

Characteristics of First- Through Third-Graders

- More interested in real life tasks, less interested in fantasy
- Fascinated by rules
- Tend to develop games with extensive rules or rituals
- Skilled at using small tools
- Enjoy tests of strength and balance
- Enjoy copying designs
- May reverse printed letters such as b and d
- Enjoy building
- May take great interest in reading
- Like magic tricks
- Enjoy collecting
- Know right from left
- Understand time and days of the week
- May double vocabulary from age 6 to 8
- Begin to separate by gender
- Self-centered, but begin to develop empathy
- Fear failure
- May have a best friend and an enemy

Continued on next page

Characteristics of Fourth- through Six-Graders

- Develop a sense of self
- Enjoy secret codes, language and rituals to strengthen friendships
- Resist supervision but become fearful without it
- Enjoy reading fiction and how-to books
- Dream about the future
- Understand concepts without as much direct experience
- Begin to see adults as fallible
- Take interest in competitive sports
- May defy authority
- Mature unequally, with girls two years more physically advanced
- Concerned about fairness
- May enjoy pleasing adults

Characteristics of Middle Schoolers

- Increased capacity for abstract thinking
- Begin to finish projects rather than just start them
- Increased memory capacity
- Improved ability to work in groups
- Can translate higher order thinking into caring and ethics
- Need to express problems and feelings
- Develop self-image as "workers"
- Take more interest in peers of opposite sex
- Seek independence but crave peer acceptance
- Become easily self-conscious
- Less concerned with daydreams of the future, more with present acceptance
- Stand up to adults
- May frequently use sarcasm
- Feel worldly
- Increase in ability to delay gratification

- Change loyalties among friends less frequently
- Look for role models other than parents
- Experience mood swings
- Value autonomy

Characteristics of High Schoolers

- Can think abstractly
- Capable of "walking in another person's shoes"
- Actively seek parents' approval
- View adult opinions as valid and acceptable while maintaining that their own views are equally as valid and acceptable
- Reduced dependence on others for thinking through problems
- Require privacy
- Seek independence
- Challenge authority figures
- Question old values
- Use peer group to test ideas and compare growth
- May join a clique, gang or club
- May show risk-taking behavior
- Need to avoid appearing trivial or childish
- Experience dramatic physical changes
- Goes through stages of awkwardness in terms of appearance and physical coordination
- Express and receive intimate or sexual advances
- Are self-conscious
- Prize friendship and loyalty
- Value intimacy
- Gain increased personal mobility
- Develop ability to adapt
- Move toward more mature sense of identity and purpose
- Distinguish between morality and legality

Checklist for Varying Your Instruction

Instructions:

1. Look over your lesson plans for the day and check the boxes that apply.
2. Check new boxes every morning for a week.
3. At the end of the week, see how much you varied your approach to engage all learners. Try to have checked one or more boxes in each set.
4. Repeat this self-test periodically until varying your instruction becomes natural.

Set 1: Linguistic Activities

☐ I will ask students to read aloud.

☐ I will assign oral presentations.

☐ I will incorporate storytelling, creative writing or word games into the day.

Set 2: Musical-Rhythmic Activities

☐ I will incorporate singing, whistling or rapping into the curriculum.

☐ I will incorporate clapping or other rhythmic activities.

☐ I will play recorded music related to the content.

Set 3: Bodily-Kinesthetic Activities

☐ I will provide hands-on experiences in which students use manipulative materials.

☐ I will ask students to role-play or act out events.

☐ I will offer opportunities for physical activities such as sports, dance or relaxation exercises.

Set 4: Interpersonal Activities

☐ I will assign group work.

☐ I will involve students in class discussions.

☐ I will encourage participation from classroom helpers.

Set 5: Spatial Intelligence

☐ I will use visual aids to enhance a lesson.

☐ I will use a metaphor to introduce a concept.

☐ I will engage students in art activities.

Set 6: Logical-Mathematical Activities

☐ I will challenge students with problem-solving tasks.

☐ I will include numbers games or activities that require calculations.

☐ I will assign science experiments.

Set 7: Intrapersonal Activities

☐ I will allow time for quiet, independent study.

☐ I will offer an assignment with several different options for study.

☐ I will encourage self-evaluation through journal writing.

Learning Bank

Student's Name: _____ Date: _____

Subject: _____

Describe what you learned and how you used the new information in your life outside of school.

Deposits
(What I learned)

Dividends
(How I drew new skills from my learning
and used them in my life)

_____   _____

_____   _____

_____   _____

_____   _____

_____   _____

Student's Signature: _____

Learning Bank

Student's Name: _____ Date: _____

Subject: _____

Describe what you learned and how you used the new information in your life outside of school.

Deposits
(What I learned)

Dividends
(How I drew new skills from my learning
and used them in my life)

_____   _____

_____   _____

_____   _____

_____   _____

Signature: _____

Web Project Resource Sites

Blue Web'n
www.kn.pacbell.com/wired/bluewebn/

A searchable database of Internet learning sites categorized by subject area, audience and type (lessons, activities, projects, resources, references and tools). Sponsored by Pacific Bell.

Earth Day Groceries Project
www.earthdaybags.org/

Yearly environmental awareness project for students.

Education World
www.education-world.com/projects/

An online journal with projects ranging from classroom e-mail exchange to those linking students by voice and video.

The Educators Toolkit
www.eagle.ca/~matin

Provides links to teacher resources, technology sites, lesson plans and Safety Net Newsletter

Electronic Emissary
www.tapr.org/emissary/

A University of Texas site bringing together students, teachers and subject matter for facilitated telementoring.

Federal Resources for Educational Excellence (FREE)
www.ed.gov/free

Offers access to hundreds of teaching and learning resources across the federal government, from historical documents and scientific experiments to mathematical challenges and famous paintings. The site supports partnerships between federal agencies and teachers to develop additional resources.

Forefront Curriculum
www.4forefront.com/intproj.html

Lists Web sites that can help teachers to integrate the Internet into the classroom. Includes a link to Internet seminars.

Global Classroom's Project Resources for Educators
www.globalclassroom.org/resource.html

Provides links to dozens of valuable sites for educators, including projects sites.

Global Grocery List Project
www.schoollife.net/schools/ggl

Sponsored by The Landmark Project, a simple activity asking the question "How much does food cost in your town?" An ongoing program in its ninth year.

The Global Schoolhouse
www.gsn.org/

Dozens of projects you can join—including international projects—hosted by numerous organizations. Sponsored by Lightspan.com.

The Globe Program
www.globe.gov/

Daily environmental measurements taken by students all over the world and shared via the Internet. Project administered by a Federal interagency team.

Holocaust/Genocide Project
www.iearn.org/iearn/hgp/

An international, nonprofit, telecommunications project to promote education and awareness. A project of the International Education and Resource Network (I*EARN).

The Jason Project
www.jasonproject.org

Annual interactive field trips—all with an online interactive component—to such locales as a volcano in Hawaii, the Galapagos Islands and the Mayan ruins. Sponsored by The JASON Foundation for Education, a nonprofit educational organization.

Journey North
www.learner.org/jnorth/

A global study of wildlife migration sponsored by The Annenberg/CPB Math and Science Project.

Judi Harris' Virtual Architecture: Designing and Directing Curriculum-Based Telecomputing
ccwf.cc.utexas.edu/~jbharris/Virtual-Architecture/index.html

Judi Harris, of the University of Texas at Austin, has put together a listing of exemplary network-based educational activities. Click on "Curriculum-Based Telecomputing Projects and Resources."

KIDLINK's Kidproj
www.kidlink.org/KIDPROJ/projects.html

Offers links to many projects of an educational or informative nature.

Midlink Magazine
www.cs.ucf.edu/~MidLink/

An electronic magazine created by students for students in the middle grades.

Monster Exchange Project
www.win4edu.com/minds-eye/monster/

A worldwide collaborative Internet e-mail project with emphasis on descriptive writing skills.

Continued on next page

Web Project Resource Sites
Continued from previous page

NickNacks' Telecollaborate!
*www.home.talkcity.com/
academydr/nicknacks/*

Dozens of links to collaborative
projects, plus tips on participating
in, developing and leading them.

Nonprofit Prophets
*www.kn.pacbell.com/wired/
prophets*

Connects students with experts to
learn more about a community or
global problem, which is then
presented along with possible
solutions in a student-designed Web
site. Sponsored by Pacific Bell.

Organization for Community Networks
www.ofcn.org/

Site hosting the Academy
TeleOlympics project, a one-day
sports competition with schools'
results posted on the Web.
Sponsored by the Organization
for Community Networks, a
nonprofit corporation in Ohio.

Save the Beaches
*ednhp.hartford.edu/www/Nina/
Beaches2.html*

A world-wide project to increase
environmental awareness and to
ensure clean beaches. Developed
by an educational computing
teacher in Connecticut.

The Teacher's Exchange
*www.teachersworkshop.com/
twshop/exchange.html*

State-by-state listings leading to
e-mail exchanges between students
or other projects of joint interest. Also
links to sites in Australia, Canada
and China.

TERC
www.terc.edu/

A nonprofit organization that
maintains links to a variety of
projects involving students in
collaborative online science
investigations.

xcitement,
g about the
y bus rides

rs-Corner/

A monthly session in which students
ages 10 to 15 meet on the Web
and write together.

Youth in Action Network
www.mightymedia.com/login.htm

Provides instruction and
participation on positive social
action and service projects on
issues such as the environment and
human rights. Sponsored by Mighty
Media, Inc., a privately funded
consortium with corporate, nonprofit
and community partnerships.

Classroom Cut-ups

Instructions:

Riddles can help students think creatively, expand their vocabularies and stretch their problem-solving and critical thinking skills. Here are a few riddles to put in your "riddle box" and use periodically. Add other riddles from library books or newspapers, if you like.

To get started, photocopy the riddles on these pages, cut them out and put them in a box. Whenever you need to fill a spare moment, have a few students draw from the riddle box and read their questions aloud. Make sure the students allow time for guessing before reading the answers.

Q. Why don't anteaters get sick?
A. They're full of little "anty" bodies.

Q. Why did the hungry boy go to the beach?
A. To eat the sand which's there.

Q. What kind of cars do farmers drive?
A. Cornvertibles.

Q. What letter does not appear in the alphabet?
A. The one you find in your mailbox.

Q. Where does the king keep his armies?
A. Up his sleevies.

Q. What walks around wearing fourteen pairs of woolen socks on its back?
A. A sheep.

Q. What is the longest word in the English language?
A. Smiles. There's a mile between the two "S"s.

Q. When do doctors become the most angry?
A. When they lose their patients.

Q. What is the smallest room in the world?
A. A mushroom.

Q. Why is a dog the best-dressed animal?
A. He wears a coat and tails—and pants.

Q. Why did the boy throw the clock out the window?
A. To see time fly.

Q. What can run for hundreds of years without getting tired?
A. A river.

Q. Why did the football coach go the bank?
A. He wanted his quarter back.

Q. What vegetable do you get when King Kong walks through your garden?
A. Squash.

Q. If a cow just had a baby, what kind of cow is she?
A. Decaffeinated.

Q. What do you get when you cross a telephone with a very big football player?
A. A wide receiver

Continued on next page

Classroom Cut-ups

Continued from previous page

Q. What do you have when 100 rabbits stand in a row and 99 step back?
A. A receding hare line.

Q. What is a sailor's favorite candy?
A. Lifesavers.

Q. What time is it when an elephant sits on a fence?
A. Time to get a new fence.

Q. What does a gambler call heaven?
A. Pair-of-dice.

Q. Why did the turtle cross the road?
A. To get to the Shell station.

Q. How does a mother hen feel when her chicks hatch?
A. Eggstatic.

Q. What do you call a boomerang that doesn't come back?
A. A stick.

Q. When is a door not a door?
A. When it's ajar.

Q. What do you call a pig's leash?
A. A hamstring.

Q. What has four wheels and flies?
A. A garbage truck.

Q. Why do bodybuilders work out on the beach?
A. They're looking for muscles.

Q. Why was Six afraid of Seven?
A. Because Seven eight Nine.

Q. Why does the guitar player choose her songs carefully?
A. She's very picky.

Q. What do you get if you cross a centipede and a parrot?
A. A walkie talkie.

Q. What always goes up but never comes down?
A. Your age.

Q. How did the queen bee fix her hair?
A. With a honeycomb.

Q. What is a park ranger's favorite dessert?
A. Chocolate moose.

Q. Why can't a hand be 12 inches.
A. Because then it would be a foot.

Q. Why did the elephant prefer driving a car to taking a bus?
A. He needed the trunk space.

Q. What's worse than finding a worm in your apple?
A. Finding half a worm.

Q. Why do fish make poor students?
A. They hang around in schools but they never study.

Q. What can you put in a milk jug to make it lighter?
A. A hole.

Continued on next page

Classroom Cut-ups

Continued from previous page

Q. What word becomes shorter when you add two letters?

A. Short.

Q. What did one wall say to the other wall?

A. I'll meet you at the corner.

Q. If a rooster laid an egg at the top of a pointed roof, which side would it roll down?

A. Neither. Roosters don't lay eggs.

Q. What has legs but cannot walk?

A. A table.

Q. Why did the tug boat follow the tanker?

A. He was looking for a solid friend-ship.

Q. What has feet but cannot run?

A. A yardstick.

Q. What do you get when you cross a railroad track with a car?

A. If the red light is flashing, you get a ticket.

Q. What has a tongue but cannot talk?

A. A shoe.

Q. Name a place where one follows twelve.

A. On a clock.

Q. What has four eyes but cannot see?

A. Mississippi.

Q. What do you get when you cross a gallon jar of pickles with a jumbo hot fudge sundae?

A. Sick.

Q. Why did the golfer bring two pair of pants to the golf course?

A. He was afraid he'd get a hole in one.

Q. What kind of music does Santa listen to while he wraps gifts?

A. Wrap music.

Q. Why did the rocket lose its job?

A. It got fired.

Q. Why was the alphabet so laid back?

A. It wanted to catch some Zs.

Q. A nickel and a dime stood on top of the Empire State Building. The nickel jumped off but the dime didn't. Why not?

A. The dime had more cents.

Q. What weighs almost nothing but can't be held for long?

A. Your breath.

Q. How long will a nine-day clock run without winding?

A. It won't run at all.

Q. When you buy this kind of rug, you get taken to the cleaners. What is it?

A. A Laundromat.

Q. What runs around the whole backyard and never moves?

A. A fence.

Q. What food is both cold and hot?

A. A brrrrr-ito.

Q. What kind of bank needs no money?

A. A river bank.

Create a Test Using Bloom's Taxonomy

Design tests that measure the depth of your students' understanding. Include six types of questions on each test. Start with basic questions that assess knowledge of the content. Add essay questions that measure students' ability to meet the broader learning objectives, such as exercising critical thinking skills and using their new knowledge. This type of assessment will help you focus your future review lessons and activities to help students more fully grasp the concepts.

The random sample questions below show how to adapt the cues according to grade level and content area. Reproduce the "Test-Maker's Worksheet" on page 164 to create your own tests.

Levels of Understanding	Sample Test Questions
1. Knowledge: Basic recall of terms, facts, concepts. Cues: List, name, define	List the first four Presidents of the United States. Name the parts of a flower. Define "estuary."
2. Comprehension: Can relate meaning, interpret and restate. Cues: Explain, summarize, paraphrase	Why was Galileo executed? Summarize the events that led to the Revolutionary War. Tell, in your own words, what the boy in the story felt after his father left.
3. Application: Can use material learned in the real world. Cues: Demonstrate, use, produce	Demonstrate how you would multiply to find out how many crayons are in the box. Show how to use four parts of speech by writing a sentence that includes a verb, a noun, an adjective and an adverb. Produce a drawing of a machine that uses a pulley, a piston, or ball bearing. Use arrows to show how it works. Classify the animals in the picture by writing "A" next to each amphibian and "R" next to each reptile.

Continued on next page

Test-Maker's Worksheet

Levels of Understanding	Sample Test Questions
1. **Knowledge:** Basic recall of terms, facts, concepts. Cues: List, name, define	
2. **Comprehension:** Can relate meaning, interpret and restate. Cues: Explain, summarize, paraphrase	
3. **Application:** Can use material learned in the real world. Cues: Demonstrate, use, produce	
4. **Analysis:** Understands elements and how they fit together. Cues: Classify, distinguish, differentiate	
5. **Synthesis:** Can combine concepts into a unified, unique whole. Cues: Combine, reorganize, relate	
6. **Evaluation:** Can judge a scenario, situation or object by applying logical criteria. Cues: Evaluate, appraise, justify, judge, defend	

Rubric

Project:

Aspects of Performance	Levels of Mastery			

CHAPTER 5

How to Establish a Classroom Community

" Our Community Circle has broken down barriers in a very mixed classroom. I make it a safe place, where every student gets a chance to speak. We discuss problems and help each other solve them. Every day I learn a little more about what make kids tick. "

One of the most profound moments for some teachers occurs when a student inadvertently calls them "Mom" or "Dad." Suddenly those teachers realize the importance of the role they play for their students.

Indeed, the classroom community serves the function of a family for several hours in a student's daily life, and the teacher sets the tone for the kind of support each student will feel in this "home away from home." You may think you teach individual students, but in reality, the quality of their individual learning often reflects the nature of their group dynamics and the atmosphere you create in the classroom community.

Just as a family works better when every member feels a sense of belonging, your students will learn more effectively when they all feel accepted and safe, despite their differences. Students learn at a higher level when the atmosphere encourages them to take risks and share their ideas without fear of ridicule or censure. They relate more effectively when they understand and agree to a set of core values that transcend personal differences.

This chapter offers strategies for building a classroom community where each student feels secure and senses his or her value to the "family"—an environment that nurtures the learning process for every student.

5

Create Connections with Students

When students feel special, they live up to that expectation. They perform well when their self-image supports the idea that they are worthwhile, capable human beings. Your interest in each student can convey this message. Even students from supportive home environments need to know that you care about their success. Those who lack support need your encouragement even more. In fact, one caring adult can make all the difference for a student experiencing trouble, and often that adult is a teacher.

The better you know each student, the better you can respond individually to each student while building a network of strong classroom relationships. Early in the year, take an inventory of student interests. You may do this in a number of ways:

- Call each student at home before school begins or send a special card or note to express that you're looking forward to having that student in your class.

- Find out about your students' interests early in the year. Incorporate students' special interests into your lesson plans throughout the year when you see opportunities to do so. This might mean something as simple as setting up math story problems that incorporate students' hobbies, or something as elaborate as having students teach the class their unique skills. If some students love baseball, you might set up a history lesson with a story about baseball. (For example: The bases were loaded and the last player struck out. That's what it must have felt like for the country that lost the war they had come so close to winning.)

- Set a special time to talk with students before or after school, and take advantage of spontaneous opportunities to ask about their families, their hobbies, their feelings about various issues and their activities outside of school.

- Take an inventory of student interests using one of the forms provided in Chapter 1 on pages 41 and 42.

Develop Trust-based Relationships

Have you ever noticed how a small child will jump into a pool and into a parent's waiting arms, while a sibling a year or two older will shy away from the edge of the pool, knowing that deep water may represent danger? The same trend occurs in the classroom. As children grow old enough to experience the learning environment, they sometimes lose their innate trust in the safety of "jumping in." They come to fear humiliation if they make a mistake or ask a "stupid" question. They begin to expect the teacher to grade them down or simply think poorly of them if they respond to a question with an idea that sounds far-fetched.

You have the power to help students find a safe haven and to assure them that you see trial and error as part of the learning process. From the very first day, you can convey that your students can trust you to accept them and support their learning. The following tips offer direct and indirect ways to do so.

Create Student-to-Teacher Trust

Safety in the classroom means feeling nurtured and protected. It means expecting to feel comfortable in the classroom—and having that expectation consistently met.

You can do a number of things to help students develop trust in you and in each other. First, recognize that students each bring different life experiences into the classroom. Do not expect every student to react to the classroom environment in the same way. Occasionally you may find a student who has absorbed negative feelings from parents who did not have a positive school experience. The student may act out or withdraw in response to an inherent mistrust of teachers or a fear of school.

You can learn a lot from listening to your students, but you may never know all the sources of a student's lack of trust. You can only do your best to develop a trusting relationship with each student and to foster an atmosphere of trust within the classroom community. Apply the following practices to develop mutual trust with individual students.

- As often as possible, address students by name. Let them know that you recognize each student as a valuable individual. Respond with an open mind to their perspectives, opinions and feelings.

- Pay attention to your students' moods. When you see that a student is struggling or seems upset, a pat on the back or a word of concern may reverse the mood. Showing an interest in students whether there is a problem or not will communicate sincerity and help them to believe that you care about their personal well-being.

- Focus on students' strengths and positive qualities.

- When a student who is often difficult has a good day, call that student at home to offer your congratulations. Call the student after a bad day to get things back on track.

- When a student comes to you with a problem, try to empathize and listen without judging. Encourage classmates to do the same for each other.

- When a student is ill, call home to ask how he or she is feeling. If the student has an extended illness, send a card. (For early elementary students, use the "Sorry You're Not Feeling Well" card provided in the resource section at the end of this chapter.)

- Help students feel accepted by allowing them to offer their ideas without feeling they have to know "the right answer."

Sorry You're Not Feeling Well
Page 184

Promote Student-to-Student Trust

Help students understand the nature of their interdependence. Point out that when someone in the room feels sad or upset, he or she communicates that feeling to others. Likewise, when someone feels comfortable and happy, it puts others at ease. Everyone learns better when students feel supported and happy in the classroom environment. Try these strategies to help students develop trusting relationships with each other.

- Convey to the class that everyone has the right to learn in a safe, peaceful environment. Explain that all students can contribute to this environment by observing the rules of safety and consideration for others.

- Emphasize the importance of each class member's right to express ideas and opinions. Establish a policy of making only constructive, never derogatory, remarks about another student's comments or class work.

- If you teach younger grades, develop a song or routine that will help create a cohesive mood in the classroom. When the mood in the classroom feels tense, have students sing the song or recite the rhyme to shift the mood.

- If you teach middle school students, you may prefer the following "Raise a Red Flag" activity.

Activity Idea:
Raise a Red Flag

1. Place a mailbox with a red flag somewhere near your desk.

2. When a student has a bad day because of something that happened in class, he or she can put a note in the mailbox and raise the red flag. The note may include a name or may be written anonymously.

   The comment may apply to an individual interaction or to a general classroom standard. It may be something general such as, "I didn't like it when people laughed at some of the class presentations" or something specific and personal such as, "I felt upset today because Smitty laughed at my presentation."

3. When you see the red flag raised, check the mailbox and decide how to address the student's concerns. If the note indicates the student's name, you may want to hold a personal discussion after school and encourage the student to have a conversation with the other parties involved. However, in some cases, you may want to initiate a general class discussion to address the topic with the whole class.

   If you hold a class discussion, raise the issue in a way that allows students to reaffirm their class values without incriminating any one student. The value of the red flag lies in the students' ability to express fears and concerns with confidentiality. Remember to honor that trust.

5

Start a Community Circle

You can help build trust among students by conducting a "community circle." Set aside time every day for students to talk through issues important to the group. Students will come to look forward to this time as an occasion to raise their concerns and share their ideas. You can discuss issues raised in the "red flag" activity described on the previous page. You can also use this as a daily opportunity to teach and promote positive social skills.

Plan the Community Circle at the same time every day. You may want to hold it first thing in the morning. That way, students who feel troubled by an incident that occurred on the way to school can get it out in the open rather than worrying about it all day. You may also find advantages to holding the Community Circle in the early afternoon to deal with issues that arise during lunch. A late afternoon session gives students a chance to celebrate the day's successes.

Plan objectives for your daily discussion ahead of time, but allow for the possibility that students will offer input that changes the direction of the discussion.

For Younger Students:

Provide a ball or other prop to encourage shy students to talk and verbose students to relinquish the floor. Each student holds the object and speaks for a certain amount of time before passing it on.

As an alternative prop, try using a puppet to ask the questions and encourage students to open up. You can employ several puppets, each with a different role such as problem solving or storytelling. Use the puppets interchangeably as needed.

For Older Students:

Use the "Community Circle Discussion Starters" reproducible provided in the resource section at the end of this chapter, to choose a topic for the day or to let students choose topics. Cut the ideas into strips and have students draw them out of a fishbowl. Or you may write a different discussion starter on the board each day.

Honor Questions

Students must feel free to take intellectual risks in order to feel psychologically "safe." An often-overlooked element of trust building is the creation of a learning environment where students can ask questions—either questions about the assignment, the content, or unrelated subjects— without fear of humiliation.

Community Circle Discussion Starters
Page 185

Embrace strategies that communicate your respect for students' questions. Experiment with these strategies:

- When a student asks for clarification about the lesson content, comment, "That's a very good question" or "I'm glad you asked that" before responding. As other students hear you respond, they will feel safer about asking questions. At the end of a study period or presentation, ask students to write a question about something they did not understand. Collect the questions, thank the students for their help, and incorporate the answers into the next day's review of the content.

- If the schedule does not permit that you take the time to answer a complex question, thank the student and explain that you will write the question on the board for safekeeping. When you get a chance, come back to the question and explain its importance in helping the class identify what they still need to learn. Then take the time needed to respond to the question.

  For instance, perhaps students are working on a writing assignment. One student looks puzzled and asks, "How can you tell whether to add 's' or 'es' to make a word plural?" The teacher looks at the word the student is trying to write and helps her choose the correct spelling. Meanwhile, the teacher writes the question on the board. After the class completes the assignment, the teacher introduces the rule about plurals, asks students for responses and gives examples of words that end in "s" and "es." She thanks the student who raised the question.

Use Mistakes as Springboards for Risk-Taking

Freedom to make mistakes enhances a student's trust in the learning process and in the teacher. It increases their ability to take risks. Students will venture forth with new ideas when they anticipate support rather than criticism. Let students know that risking a guess is often better than not thinking or responding at all. Tell them that everyone—even teachers—makes mistakes. Explain that mistakes contribute to the learning process. Rather than punish or discredit students for errors, turn mistakes into group learning opportunities using this strategy:

- After a test or homework assignment, have students choose one problem they missed and still cannot figure out.

- Then ask them to meet in groups of three and collaborate to find the correct answer to each of their three questions. (If one student made no errors, another student in the group can choose a second problem for discussion.) Circulate and help those groups who feel stumped on an answer.

- Finally, have each group present to the class the question, the appropriate answer, and the explanation, without emphasizing which group member made the mistake. This exercise helps students see how their mistakes can become learning experiences for the whole class.

Encourage Shared Values

When students unite around core classroom values, they can better support one another's learning. Fairly early in the year, you may want to help students explore their beliefs about learning and understand how they can improve the classroom community by acting on those beliefs. When you think your students are ready, consider introducing the following "Identifying Core Values" activity. This approach works especially well for third graders and older. You may prefer the ideas for mottoes and banners on the next page for K–3 students.

Activity Idea: Identifying Core Values

1. Facilitate a class discussion on the question, "What qualities do we need to build a strong classroom community?"

2. List the responses on the board. Elicit qualities such as courtesy, trust, safety, and respect. Have the class vote on the four most important qualities.

3. Divide the class into four groups. Assign each group one of the qualities chosen. Ask each group to identify what their assigned quality looks like and sounds like. Use the "Qualities of a Good Classroom Community" reproducible provided in the resource section.

4. Spend some time with each group as the groups brainstorm what they would hear, see and feel when their quality is present in the classroom. For instance, if a classroom community values courtesy, students would hear each other saying "please" and "thank you." If the classroom community values safety, students would see each other calmly talking to resolve conflicts rather than hitting or hurting each other. Students can either write or draw illustrations on the worksheets.

Qualities of a Good
Classroom Community
Pages 186

5. Ask each group to write a statement to summarize the important aspects of the quality. For instance, "Courtesy helps us all participate and feel good about each other. We show courtesy by letting others have a choice or a first turn, and by speaking politely."

6. Have the groups read their final statements to the entire class. Post the papers on a bulletin board for future reference, to remind students why they all benefit when they honor class values and observe class standards.

Use Mottoes and Banners

After a class discussion on the topic of shared values, challenge students to create symbols that summarize those values.

- Develop a class motto. The class motto may be as simple as, "We all do our best by helping each other." The motto may grow out of the activity above or you may want to introduce it at the very beginning of the year. (See page 31 to make it a morning ritual.) As a variation, you may want students to determine a monthly motto to vary or add detail to the message.

- Ask students to brainstorm a symbol representing unity to use as a class logo. Or have early elementary students draw pictures to illustrate sharing, honesty or other class values. Display the symbols or drawings on the bulletin board.

- Have students create banners reflecting their class motto. They can use the symbols on the banners. You can hang the banners on the bulletin board.

- Students can use mottoes as part of a writing or journal assignment. Have them respond to a question such as, "How can I uphold the class motto?"

- Send the motto home so parents can feel like a part of the class community and reinforce the motto's implied values at home.

Break Down Seating Barriers

Location can affect relationships within the classroom community. Examples of basic seating arrangements appeared in Chapter 1. Although you may have assigned every student a seat at the first of the year you may still want to periodically evaluate the influence of the arrangements on your classroom community.

Vary your seating assignments to communicate that every student shares equal importance. Make sure students get to know a wide variety of classmates. Pay particular attention not to separate the boys from the girls. Some teachers gravitate toward male-dominated sections of the room in order to control behavior. To avoid these patterns, you may want to try one or more of the following suggestions:

- Arrange seating by drawing names randomly out of a jar.

- Seat students in groups by favorite pets, sports, foods, or colors.

- Seat alphabetically by middle names, street names or favorite names.

- If your students currently sit in rows, ask them to turn their desks and face the opposite wall, or try clustering their desks. If you currently use clusters, change the number in your groupings.

- Have students sit in a U-shape, an O-shape, a V-shape or a double-E shape.

5

Create Classroom Celebrations and Ceremonies

Teachers have discovered many ways to establish traditions that convey the importance of each student while establishing group values. Class celebrations, in particular, help reinforce a sense of unity and cooperation. They can affirm each student's sense of belonging and joy in learning together.

The following tips will help you craft a plan to celebrate each student's uniqueness, to celebrate learning, and also to build a sense of community.

- Birthdays provide ideal opportunities to celebrate an individual's uniqueness. Even older students enjoy the special recognition they may not get every day from a teacher with several classes and many students. Write a special note saying what you like about the student and have him or her stand for applause. Or you may use the reproducible "Happy Birthday" card in the resource section for younger students. You may even want to have a supply of treats ready to tuck in with each note.

  To keep track of birthdays, either record them on the "Birthday List" provided or record them directly from the students' interest inventories or information cards into your plan book. Each week, glance at the birthdays that will occur and take a couple of minutes to write a note or card for each birthday student. For students with summer birthdays, celebrate their half-birthday. (Count six months back from their birthdays.)

- If you have younger students and you hold a class party for birthdays, let the other students express gratitude for the birthday person's uniqueness. Invite students to write notes about their classmate in a "birthday book" that remains in the classroom throughout the year.

- Celebrate the completion of a class project. For instance, students who have studied the pilgrims might celebrate by holding a fair to display the colonial crafts they have learned.

- Celebrate students' individual learning. After a project in which each student chose a country and compiled data on it over the course of a unit, the class could hold a food fest featuring dishes from their individual countries.

Happy Birthday, _____ !

Your birthday is special to me
because you are special, don't you see?
We all enjoy your smiling face.
You make our classroom a better place.
So whatever is on your birthday plate,
know that Room _____ and I think you're great.

Your teacher,

_____

Happy Birthday, _____!
Page 187

BIRTHDAY LIST!

January	July
February	August
March	September
April	October
May	November
June	December

Birthday List
Page 188

- Hold ceremonies to celebrate others' contributions. A class can sponsor a parents' tea to recognize and honor the parents of students.

- Recognize achievement. Track-meet ceremonies where everyone gets an award or class ceremonies where every student receives a certificate convey that students can jointly celebrate their successes.

Help Students Validate One Another

A responsive teacher looks for opportunities to help students accept and validate one another, provide encouragement and express empathy for each other. Consider the following ideas:

- When a student is absent because of an extended illness, call the student at home and express your concern. Pass around a get-well card for the class to sign. (See page 184.)

- When a student performs in an important recital or special athletic event outside of school, try to attend the event and encourage other students to come with their parents. You might even arrange a carpool and attend as a group.

- When a student moves away, let the class members record their memories with artwork or photos to send to the student. These mementos will remind the student that classroom relationships can endure beyond the boundaries of the classroom. They can also provide comfort if the student feels lonely in his or her new school.

Capture Collective Memories

Good memories help to generate a positive feeling about the classroom community. Create a class photo album to help your students reflect on their positive interactions throughout the year. Keep disposable cameras handy or store a loaded camera so you can capture:

- Students engaged in group work.

- Students enjoying an art project or sports activity.

- Special events or field trips.

- Awards ceremonies (for appropriate behavior, homework completion, improvement).

- A visit from a special guest.

- Completion of long-range projects (photo of student with project).

- Classroom diversity (photo of each student showing special talent, hobby or best work).

- Students making oral presentation.

- Displays of student work.

If you like, you can make copies of the photos to include in student portfolios or on bulletin board displays. Make the scrapbook available on open house night and for classroom visitors to view throughout the year. Take at least one photo of each student to send home with a note at the end of the year.

5

Teach Cooperative Learning Skills

Group work provides students with important learning opportunities, but some new teachers shy away from it because of unsuccessful early experiences. You can experience the benefits of cooperative learning right from the start if you approach it with forethought and planning.

Cooperative learning benefits the individual learner as well as the learning community. Students working in groups can become hands-on participants where, in a general classroom discussion, they may be too shy to speak up. They learn social skills where, in independent work, they may feel isolated. They learn to pool their resources and expand their potential rather than limiting themselves to the knowledge they can learn on their own.

Many projects lend themselves to group work, especially those in which students need to brainstorm ideas or learn a large or complex body of information. Teams can often accomplish what no one individual could accomplish on his or her own. An ideal group project does not ask students within the group to duplicate one another's efforts but asks them to produce something new. It results in a product more comprehensive than any one member could have created alone in the same amount of time.

Use the "Jigsaw Strategy"

Have you ever wondered how to help students absorb a lot of information in a fairly brief time period? Cooperative groups let students magnify their learning while building a sense of camaraderie. Teach your students the invaluable life skills associated with group work by introducing the "jigsaw strategy." This strategy helps students learn to work interdependently as they study the lesson content.

Use jigsaw strategy to divide a complex topic into "chunks" or subtopics. Each student or group can then take responsibility for researching a subtopic and reporting back to the group. The groups then meet together to share their learning. In this way, everyone fulfills a specific responsibility and the whole class benefits from the shared knowledge.

See the examples on the facing page for ideas on how to integrate the strategy into your curriculum.

5

Sample Activities
Using the Jigsaw Strategy

Grades K–3: Letting Geometry Take Shape

Tell students to pretend they will go to a park a long distance from their homes. Ask each student to choose whether he or she will travel in a car, on a bus or on a bicycle. Have each of the students draw the vehicle he or she chose.

Ask all the students who chose the car to go to one area of the room, the students who chose the bus to go to another area, and the students who chose the bicycle to go to a third area.

Have students put their drawings alongside each other and identify the shapes (i.e., squares, rectangles, circles, triangles, diamonds or lines) that appear within the drawings. They can draw or write down the shapes on a separate page.

Let each group report the shapes they found to the entire class.

Grades 4–6: Digesting Food Groups

Assign students to work in groups of four to study the basic food groups.

Within each group, one student reads about and makes a list of dairy products, one lists fruits and vegetables, one covers breads and grains and one studies nuts, meats and legumes.

Next, students who studied like food groups meet together and form new groups. In other words, all the dairy experts meet at one table, the fruits and vegetable experts meet together, and so forth. Together, the experts see if they can expand their lists or knowledge.

Students return to their original groups and report their learning. Each group creates a balanced menu for a day, incorporating all the food groups.

Secondary Grades: Author, Author!

On the chalkboard, list the authors whose works appear in the students' literature textbook. Divide the names into three columns according to the authors' genres.

Ask each student to choose an author whose works they would like to study. Next, have each student silently read the selections by that author.

Assign students to meet in three groups: a group for Column 1 authors, another for Column 2 authors and one for Column 3 authors. Have each group compare and contrast the literary devices and styles of the authors whose works they read.

Have each group report to the class on the literary genre or time period their authors represent.

5

Lay the Groundwork for Successful Group Work

Group work has great potential to enhance student learning, but only when students exhibit the collaboration skills they need to work effectively with others. You can go a long way toward fostering these skills and helping students learn the group dynamics so necessary for success in school, in today's workplace and in society. Read Chapter 6, "How to Teach Social Skills," to find ways to help students develop the skills they need. Beyond that, you can observe the following guidelines to ensure the effectiveness of your learning groups.

- **Limit teams to four to six students.**

  Research indicates that this group size works best because it is small enough to prevent verbal domination by one student or the "ganging up" of two students by picking on another. Yet the group size is small enough to allow each student to participate.

- **Create diverse teams.**

  Mix the skills, strengths and personalities of the group members. Think of how an effective committee works. Make sure each group includes members with leadership traits, organizational skills and artistic abilities. Vary the gender and ethnicity of the groupmates as well. The variety of their perspectives will help students learn something they might not learn in a group of students with more similar life experiences.

- **Keep the teams together for several weeks.**

  The more time you give students to work together, the more they will learn to work with each other's strengths and weaknesses and to build trusting relationships. Once a team has worked through that process, they will have time to enjoy the benefits of their efforts. Vary the composition of the groups after several weeks to expand student-to-student relationships.

- **Present activities that help students get to know one another.**

  Each time you change the membership of the groups, have students interview one another about their personal interests, opinions and feelings. Write the interview questions based on the grade level and content. This important step will build trust among team members and help them develop insights into how they might best work together.

- **Help members create a team identity.**

  Challenge each group to come up with a tag line or logo or to conduct another activity that will lead to cohesiveness.

- **Teach high standards and goals for group work.**

  Ask that each group develop a set of standards for their interactions. Each member should agree to:

  — Help each other.

  — Share materials and information.

  — Take turns and avoid interrupting.

  — Praise one another.

  — Talk quietly so as not to disturb other groups.

Our Group Constitution
Page 189

You may want each group to create a constitution based on its standards for interaction. Or use the reproducible sample "Our Group Constitution" in the resource section.

Help Students Celebrate Group Success

Groups work best when students support each other and truly celebrate one another's success. You can encourage cooperation and appreciation and minimize competition by designing projects that emphasize group goals. Preview the following examples to adapt an idea for your class.

- After a series of oral presentations, have students write positive reviews indicating what they appreciated about each presentation.

- In PE class, ask students to shoot baskets with the goal of scoring a certain number of points collectively, rather than pitting two teams against one another. Or ask students to see how many times they can pass a volleyball across the net without dropping it.

- Set up a group project in which individuals do not receive their grades until everyone in the group has contributed his or her part. If everyone meets the deadline, the whole group gets extra points. Students will feel an incentive to help one another and to congratulate one another at the completion of the project.

- Hold a reading contest in which the class tries to achieve a group goal rather than having individuals vie for the most books read. For instance, if the class reads 50 books combined, they can have a party. For 75 books, they can attend a special field trip.

5

Assign Study Buddies

Working in small groups can enhance learning and camaraderie. The "study buddy" concept goes one step further. It helps students take personal responsibility for each other. You can assign study buddies at the first of the year to promote long-term relationships based on mutual concern. Follow these suggestions to incorporate study buddies into your classroom community.

- Remind students that each one of them can contribute to the classroom community in important ways. Explain that one of these ways is to think of the needs of someone else. That's when study buddies become important.

- Explain that each study buddy is responsible for collecting papers and keeping track of assignments when his or her buddy is absent. Study buddies can also get together when one of them is stuck on a problem or needs an idea.

Be My Buddy
Page 190

- Have the study buddies exchange phone numbers. They can also call each other if they need clarification on homework assignments. Use the "Be My Buddy" reproducible provided in the resource section.

- When a student is absent, arrange a time at the beginning of the day for the student to meet with his or her study buddy to go over the missed work.

- When a new student enters the class, assign the newcomer a study buddy right away. The study buddy can help the new student adjust by explaining procedures for keeping track of assignments and turning in work.

Study buddies also come in handy when you need students to be responsible for each other. On field trips, fire drills and other occasions, ask study buddies to pair up. A student may feel less likely to stray when asked to help a partner stay with the group.

Variation for Older Students:

Middle-school students can benefit from study buddies, but be careful not to take the onus off the absent student for keeping track of missed assignments. You might want to assign three or four study buddies to each student and have the absent buddy call the others to find out about the assignments. This way, if one buddy isn't home, the absent student has two more buddies to rely on and no excuses to make.

Activity Idea:
A Close-Knit Class of Study Buddies

Study buddies encourage students to look beyond themselves and see the importance of another person in the classroom community. Encourage this "other-directedness" by creating a patchwork-quilt bulletin board representing the class community.

- Give each student a copy of the "Our Patchwork Quilt" reproducible provided in the resource section.

- Tell the class that each student is like a beautiful patch on a quilt, and so the class will create a paper quilt on the bulletin board. Each patch will feature an illustration of a class member, but instead of making self-portraits, each student will draw his or her study buddy, emphasizing the buddy's best qualities.

- Underneath the portraits, students will explain why their study buddies are important members of the class.

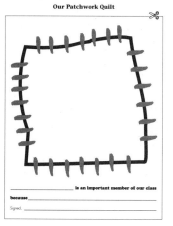

Our Patchwork Quilt
Page 191

Dear _____,

Sorry you're not feeling well.
We miss you!

From your classmates in room _____

and _____
Teacher's signature

Community Circle Discussion Starters

Use the following discussion starters to encourage communication in a Community Circle.

- I really get angry when…
- I am happy when…
- The funniest thing I ever saw was…
- If I saw a friend calling someone a name…
- The best time I had with my family was…
- My friend and I…
- When I grow up…
- If I could run the family…
- If I could run the classroom…
- I care about people who…
- When someone pushes me around I…
- I feel left out when…
- How I feel today is…
- One thing that happened in the last 24 hours that made me feel great is…
- I am proud of…
- One thing I am very good at is…
- I wish…
- A nice thing I did once for someone was…
- A nice thing someone did once for me was…
- My wish for today is…
- The scariest thing that ever happened to me was. . .
- My favorite place to visit is…
- The holiday I like best is…
- My favorite game is…
- After school I like to…
- The best gift I ever got was…
- My favorite TV show is…
- A nice thing that happened to me today is…
- When I'm alone I like to…
- My favorite color is…
- Being a friend means…
- I am proud of…
- Today I wish…
- Today I want…

- Today I will…
- One thing I look forward to is…
- My most special possession is…
- What I like best about my class is…
- A special memory I have is…
- My favorite thing to do with friends is…
- One nice thing I like to do with my family is…
- The most difficult thing I ever did was…
- One thing I would like to change about myself is…
- If I needed a safe place to go to think or to be alone, I would go…
- One change I have made this year that I feel proud of is…
- Something I lost that was important or special to me was…
- It is the beginning of a new year. What can each of you do to help make our classroom or school a safer place?
- You and your friends stopped by a snack place after school. You ordered juice but were served a soda. What will you do about it?
- What is one thing you dislike doing most? Why? What can you do about it?
- What is one thing you would like to do but need help from someone else to do it?
- Did you ever feel that you did not like someone when you first met him or her? Why? Did you change your mind? If you did, why did you?
- Do you like spending time alone or would you rather be with friends? Why?
- What do you look for in a friend? Do you choose a friend because of looks? Brains? Kindness or loyalty? Fun? Other reasons?

Add some of your own "starters":

- _____
- _____
- _____
- _____
- _____

Qualities of a Good Classroom Community

A good classroom community has the following quality: _____.

Describe this quality below. What would we see, hear and feel in the classroom if this quality was present?

Looks like:	Sounds like:	Feels like:
1.		
2.		
3.		

Summary Statement:

_____

_____

_____

_____

_____

_____

_____

_____

_____

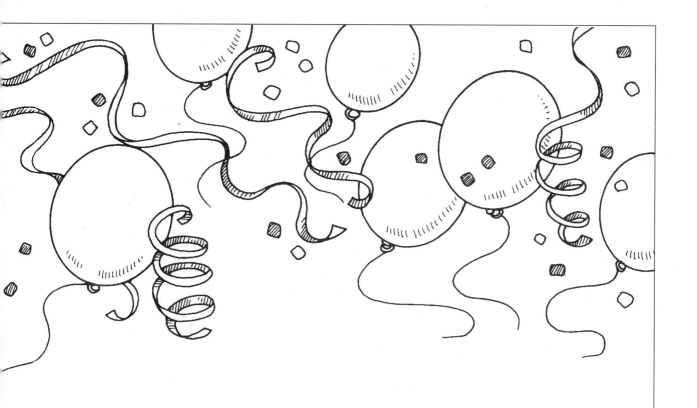

Happy Birthday, _____ !

Your birthday is special to me

because you are special, don't you see?

We all enjoy your smiling face.

You make our classroom a better place.

So whatever is on your birthday plate,

know that Room _____ and I think you're great.

Your teacher,

_____

January

February

March

April

May

June

July

August

September

October

November

December

Our Group Constitution

We believe that all group members are created equal.

We will show that we appreciate the contributions of every member.

When a group member speaks, we will listen without interrupting.

We will all do our share of the work.

We will all help each other, knowing that we depend on each other for group success.

Be My Buddy

Be My Buddy

To: _____

From: _____

Hi. I'm your study buddy.

Call me if you are sick or need to discuss our homework.

You can reach me at: _____

Be My Buddy

To: _____

From: _____

Hi. I'm your study buddy.

Call me if you are sick or need to discuss our homework.

You can reach me at: _____

Be My Buddy

To: _____

From: _____

Hi. I'm your study buddy.

Call me if you are sick or need to discuss our homework.

You can reach me at: _____

Be My Buddy

To: _____

From: _____

Hi. I'm your study buddy.

Call me if you are sick or need to discuss our homework.

You can reach me at: _____

Our Patchwork Quilt

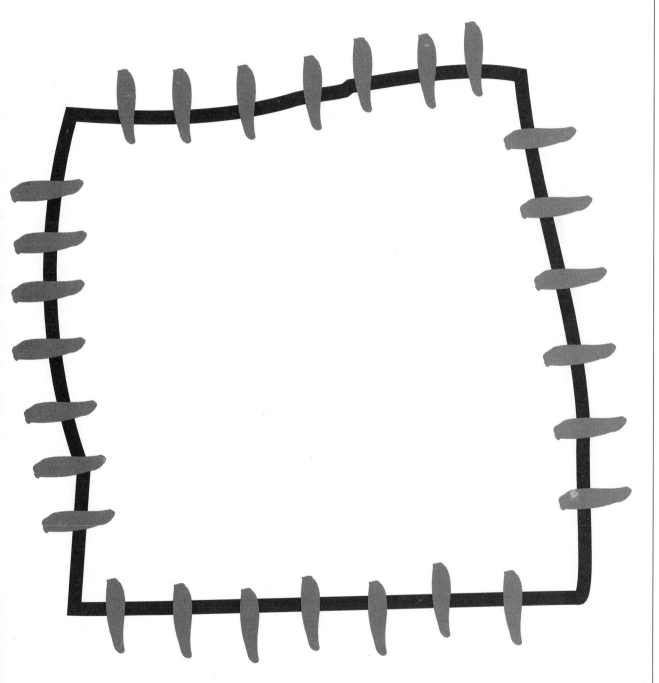

_____ **is an important member of our class**

because_____

Signed, _____

CHAPTER 6

How to Teach Social Skills

" I have a great class, but some of my kids acted so tough at first. I actually had to teach them what caring about other people is all about—what you do, how you show it. Now they really try to work on their anger and the whole class is more relaxed and positive. "

Some new teachers enter the classroom expecting to find students who treat others with kindness and courtesy. They often discover that too many students lack the prior training to know how to cope with frustration, control anger and respect the rights of others.

The social climate in your classroom will influence every student's learning and well-being, and the development of prosocial behavior will promote a student's success throughout life. Successful teachers quickly learn the importance of teaching social skills, and now that you've become a teacher, you have inherited the job of role model and social mentor.

"Many of my students don't know how to relate to other students," one teacher reported. "They have a difficult time cooperating, sharing, taking turns or displaying empathy for others. When they don't get their way, they punch, hit, shove and call each other names.

"So I begin the year by setting prosocial expectations for my students, such as 'Listen without interrupting,' 'No put-downs,' and 'Keep hands and feet to yourself.' Then I actively teach what those rules mean, along with the social skills that children need to get along. And I reinforce and reinforce and reinforce. I look for teachable moments to praise students for sharing, taking turns or other helping behaviors."

This teacher learned the importance of offering students a vocabulary of social skills. You may find, as she did, that as you teach your students prosocial behavior, *your* job will become much easier. The time you invest teaching these behaviors can save time spent later administering discipline and soothing hurt feelings. This chapter will help you consider the many ways you can teach and reinforce social skills. The activities provided will help you create a concrete plan.

6

Teach by Explanation and Example

Consider yourself a molder of human character. As you teach students reading, math, science, history and art, for example, you also teach them kindness, courtesy, respect and, in general, the art of getting along with people. These "people skills" may determine students' success in life as much or more than their knowledge of the lesson content.

You can teach social skills in many ways. In fact, many teachers do so inadvertently, without realizing how much students absorb by watching and listening to the teacher. Although a good example is perhaps the most powerful teaching strategy, no one method stands alone. Teachers help students learn prosocial attributes most effectively with a combination of:

- **Formal presentation.**

  Students learn best when you deliberately teach them a vocabulary of social skills and show them how to practice those skills. The suggestions in this chapter will help you design lessons to teach good manners, the art of compliments, empathy, listening skills, appreciation of differences, anger management and effective negotiation.

- **Teacher modeling.**

  When teachers establish a caring, respectful attitude, it sets a standard for students. Conversely, students can also absorb negative or critical attitudes from their teachers. Try to reflect the attributes you want your students to emulate. For example, if you want your students to treat each other with respect and not call attention to one another's faults, make sure you never criticize and humiliate your students. If you want students to develop good manners, take care that you express your appreciation and exemplify kindness. If you want to teach anger management, show patience and restraint in your interactions.

- **Teachable moments.**

  You will find many spontaneous opportunities to teach social skills. You might see a student interaction in progress and step in to suggest an appropriate response. Or in your own one-on-one conversations, you may help a student rephrase a comment. Look for teachable moments like the examples listed below:

  – When you see two students arguing over a marker, take the opportunity to teach them how to share.

  – When you see one student picking on another, teach empathy to help the student understand that teasing hurts.

  – When you see a student become frustrated and react with hostility, seize the chance to teach anger management.

6

- **Teacher expectations.**

  When you discuss your class rules, introduce and demonstrate the skills needed for students to follow those rules. For instance, when teaching students how to work together in groups, discuss the importance of sharing. Have students role-play sharing materials, information and ideas.

- **Reinforcement through academic curriculum.**

  In some schools, teachers reinforce the vocabulary of social skills by examining events in history, motivations of historical figures and attributes of story characters. In this way, even your content can extend the discussion of social skills. For instance, after reading a story, you may ask students to name the qualities of the main characters and imagine how their actions and attributes influenced the outcome. Similarly, the study of a war can generate a discussion about negotiation skills or a hypothetical analysis of what would happen if the leaders of both sides had used more empathy or compassion.

- **Resources for reinforcement outside the classroom.**

  Many parents welcome ideas that help them teach social skills at home. The books recommended on pages 115 to 118, whether used at home, in the library or in the classroom, will reinforce social sensitivity and character development.

This chapter focuses mostly on social skills concepts for direct instruction and practice. It offers ideas around which you can build a lesson plan and follow-up activities throughout the year. Before you develop your lessons, assess what you have already done to lay a foundation for teaching social skills.

To assess your own efforts at promoting responsible social behavior, copy the self-test "Teaching My Students to Get Along" in the resource section at the end of the chapter. Don't worry if you find yourself checking "sometimes" or "seldom" a lot. This section is designed to help you increase your consciousness of how you influence student behavior by teaching social skills, and to offer you helpful ideas. Retake the survey in a few months to evaluate your own growth in this area.

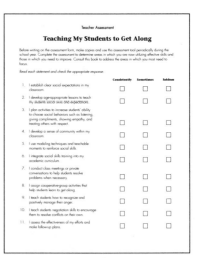

Teaching My Students to Get Along
Page 217

6

Assess Your Students' Social Skills

Once you've assessed your own teaching practices, assess the social reality your students face in the schoolyard and in the classroom. Find out the prevailing fears and expectations that may indicate a need for you to teach certain social skills throughout the classroom. Use the student survey "Getting Along in School" in the resource section to get a sense of how students think their classmates get along, as well as whether they feel safe in and around the school building and grounds. Follow these pointers:

- With younger students, adapt the questions to their level of understanding and discuss them as a group.

- Invite older students to fill out the questionnaire on their own.

- Let students answer anonymously to encourage greater honesty.

The survey can provide valuable information that will help you determine what kinds of problems students face in getting along and how best to help. Repeat the survey in a few months or midyear as a means of checking your progress in teaching prosocial skills.

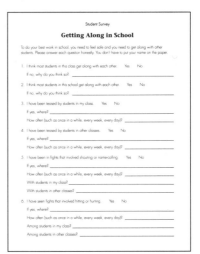

Getting Along in School
Page 218

Monitor Manners

A newspaper columnist once received a letter asking her opinion about a personal habit the letter-writer wanted to break. The columnist replied, "Manners refer to what you do when others are present. Morals refer to what you do when no one is present. My column is about manners, not morals."

Help your students see that "manners refer to what you do when others are present." Explain that every time they interact with other people, the actions they choose can show courtesy or a lack of it.

The yearlong process of teaching manners in the classroom starts with basics such as setting a standard for use of the words, "please," "thank-you," and "excuse me." Yet teaching manners also means helping students see that attitude and tone of voice can convey good manners as much as the words they choose.

For older students, courtesy includes avoiding sarcasm. For even the youngest students, it can mean using welcoming words to help everyone feel included. Before you teach the subtleties of manners, begin with the basics, then look for opportunities to expand students' awareness and definition of good manners throughout the year. You may want to use the introductory activity on the next page.

6

Activity Idea:
Good Manners

1. Distribute a snack to students as they walk into the classroom. Then say, "I counted ____ students who said 'Thank you.' I really feel good when you say thank you. It shows me that you appreciated what I did and it tells me that you know how to be polite."

2. Have students list other expressions that indicate politeness, such as "Please," "You're welcome," "Excuse me" and "I'm sorry." List these words and phrases on the board. Vary your inflection as you say the words and point out that *how* we speak matters as much as *what* we say. Have students practice using a polite tone of voice.

3. Ask students to work in pairs to role-play situations in which they must practice good manners. For instance, one student sees another carrying a heavy stack of books. The student offers to carry half the books. The other student says "Thank you."

   You may want to use puppets to role-play various situations for younger students. Older students may want to define and locate words related to good manners in the "Good Manners Word Puzzle." Or you may challenge them to develop a comic book about manners, with each student contributing one comic strip. Make copies of the "Good Manners Comic Strip." You will find both reproducibles in the resource section.

4. Review the lesson several times throughout the year. From time to time, challenge students to keep track of the number of times they say "please" or "thank you" throughout the day.

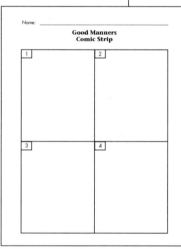

Good Manners Word Puzzle
Page 219

Good Manners Comic Strip
Page 220

6

Model the Art of Compliments

Recognize your own potential as a role model, especially in the art of giving compliments. Help students learn to define a compliment and watch for opportunities to give one. When you show students how to give compliments, they learn the habit of looking for the good in others rather than criticizing and creating classroom conflict.

Activity Idea:
Catalog Student Compliments

1. Look for the "Catalog of Compliments!" in the resource section and make a copy for each student. Also copy and cut out "You Deserve a Compliment" cards.

2. Use the cards to write a compliment to each student in the class. Before school, put one of the cards on each student's desk. A classroom aide can help read the compliments to younger students.

3. After students come in and read their compliments, ask them the following questions:

   • What is a compliment?

   • How does it feel to receive a compliment?

   • When is a good time to give a compliment?

4. Point out that it feels good to give compliments to others. Encourage students to give compliments when someone does a kind deed, accomplishes a task, or makes a genuine effort to do something positive. Explain that a person who receives a compliment should say "Thank you."

5. Give each student several copies of the "You Deserve a Compliment!" card and a copy of the "Catalog of Compliments." Ask them to refer to these compliments to consider the types of compliments they might give. Students write their compliments on a card and drop them into a Compliment Jar.

6. At the end of the day, select "compliment readers" to draw the slips from the jar and read them aloud. Ask students who benefits from compliments. Elicit the response that both the giver and the receiver feel good.

Catalog of Compliments
Page 221

You Deserve a Compliment!
Page 222

6

Create an Atmosphere of Respect

Teachers today often feel that they spend too much time resolving petty conflicts. You can reduce the number of conflicts by helping students develop basic respect for others. Teach them the concept of respect and illustrate how it applies in the classroom. Let them examine how their actions demonstrate respect for others in the classroom community. Then make respect one of your classroom standards.

Activity Idea: Define Respect

1. Ask students to brainstorm ways they do not like others to treat them—for example, when others touch their possessions or cut in front of them in line.

2. List students' statements on the board. For each statement listed, ask students how they would like to be treated. For example, they might say, "I want you to ask me whether you can borrow my eraser."

3. Next, ask them how they would want to treat others. Elicit answers such as, "If somebody said he wants me to ask before I borrow something that belongs to him, then I need to ask first."

4. Ask the class: "When we treat others the way we would like to be treated, what do we call it? Elicit the answer: We call it treating others with respect."

5. Explain the dictionary definition of respect:

   • Holding someone in high regard.

   • Showing concern.

   • Not interfering (with someone's possessions, activities or personal space).

   Challenge students to think of examples of respect that relate to their interactions at school and at home. Have them role-play, draw pictures, or write scenarios in which students can show respect.

6. Whenever you see a conflict between students that violates one of these aspects of respect, ask them to think of a more respectful way for students to treat one another.

6

Emulate Empathy

Empathy means feeling sincere concern for and understanding of others' feelings. When students develop the capacity for empathy, they make more sensitive choices about what to do and say in a given situation. True empathy indicates a high level of moral development. By modeling empathy and giving students many opportunities to practice it, you will help them instinctively develop other social skills as well. Help students see that empathy makes others feel accepted, respected and cared about. Discuss how seeing another person's point of view often helps people resolve conflicts.

Activity Idea:
Walk in Each Other's Shoes

1. Bring in two shoes from home—your favorite casual shoe and one that belongs to a family member or friend. For instance, the right shoe might be your hiking boot, running shoe or beach sandal, and the left shoe might be a toddler's or spouse's dress shoe.

2. Explain to students why you like the right shoe and describe how comfortable you feel wearing it. Then show them the left shoe belonging to someone else. Ask them to imagine how you might feel if you wore that one along with your favorite shoe. Would it feel comfortable? Could you still participate in the activities you enjoy when wearing the other shoe? Elicit the response that because feet differ, it is difficult to trade shoes with someone.

3. Explain that just as no two people have exactly the same feet, no two people have exactly the same feelings. "Trying on" another person's feelings can be as difficult as "trying on" their shoes.

4. Point out that when we try to understand someone's actions and experience their struggles or feelings of pain, people refer to it as "walking in someone else's shoes." Empathy means trying to imagine and share another person's burden— trying to "walk in someone else's shoes."

5. Generate examples of situations that call for empathy, such as when someone loses a pet, does not make the school ball team or receives teasing from a classmate. Discuss how it feels to experience these situations. For each example, ask for specific ways a student might show empathy—through comments, facial expressions or actions.

6. Discuss the difficulty of showing empathy. Remind students of the shoe-trading activity. Point out that each person's feelings are just as unique as the different shoes they wear. We cannot assume we know how someone feels. Sometimes we need to ask, then exercise good listening skills to know how best to show empathy.

7. Ask students to think of a situation in class when they could have put themselves in someone else's shoes. It may have been when another student felt embarrassed or hurt or ill. Challenge them to hold a conversation with the person they thought of and express how they would have felt given the same circumstances. Ask them to think of something they might do or say to help the student feel better.

6

Create a Test Using Bloom's Taxonomy

Continued from previous page

Levels of Understanding	Sample Test Questions
4. Analysis: Understands elements and how they fit together. Cues: Classify, distinguish, differentiate	Distinguish the difference between pine needles and redwood needles. Explain the differences in the goals and lifestyles of the pilgrims and the goals and lifestyles of the indigenous Americans in the 13 colonies. Group the beads by their shapes. Put the round ones in one pile. Put the square ones in a second pile. Put the triangles in a third pile.

5. Synthesis: Can combine concepts into a unified, unique whole.
 	
Cues: Combine, reorganize, relate
	List all the multiples of two in this group.
	
	Reorganize the list of citizens in the order of their importance to Aztec culture:
	
	  – Architects
	  – Artists and craftspeople
	  – Farmers
	  – Government leaders
	  – Religious leaders

6. Evaluation: Can judge a scenario, situation or object by applying logical criteria. Cues: Evaluate, appraise, justify, judge, defend	Judge which choice would be the fairest solution to Curious George's problem. Appraise the two stories above and tell which is the best example of a fable. Justify your choice. Based on our experiment, defend your knowledge of the movement of molecules.

Build Listening Skills

Good listeners make good learners. Most people listen without consciously thinking of the act as a skill. Teach your students to recognize the signs of effective listening and to consciously practice these behaviors.

Discuss how good it feels to know that someone is listening to you completely. Ask students to identify the signs that a person is listening. To make sure they have included everything, ask them to observe what they are doing at the moment with their own minds, voices, heads and eyes.

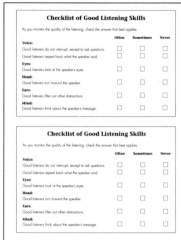

Distribute the "Checklist of Good Listening Skills" provided in the resource section. Discuss the signs of good listening. Introduce at least one of the following activities to help students practice these skills. Younger students will probably enjoy the first activity, and the second activity may be more appropriate for older students.

Checklist of Good Listening Skills
Page 223

Whichever you choose, remember to reinforce good listening skills in the weeks and months that follow the formal activity. Continually remind students what good listening looks like, sounds like and feels like. Periodically distribute copies of the listening checklist to help students reassess one another.

Activity Idea:
Sharing Stories

Distribute a copy of the "Checklist of Good Listening Skills" to each student. Have students role-play good listening skills by telling and hearing stories.

1. Group students in triads. Ask them to identify a speaker, a listener and a monitor within their groups.

2. Ask the speakers in each group to tell the plot of a favorite book or movie or to share a personal experience, while the listeners pay close attention. The monitors observe the listeners and use the checklist to assess their listening skills. The monitors then give the checklist to the listeners who reflect on their listening habits.

3. After one minute, ask students to switch roles. Let the students in each triad switch roles until everyone has had a chance to act as the speaker, the listener and the monitor.

4. In a class discussion, have students report how it felt to be a good listener and to share their ideas with a good listener.

Activity Idea:
Rate Your Listeners

1. Plan this activity when students are preparing class presentations, either individually or in small groups. Assign three students who are not presenting to serve as listening monitors and give each one a copy of the "Checklist of Good Listening Skills." After the oral presentations, ask the monitors to determine how well the audience listened to the presentation.

2. After the presentations, write the ratings on the board and have students discuss how effectively the audience listened.

3. Have students meet in small groups or in pairs to discuss the quality of the listening and how it made them feel about their performances if they gave a presentation. Ask them to reflect on what the exercise showed them about the importance of listening. Walk around the room and consult with the groups as they reflect.

4. In a class discussion, summarize the impact of good listening on every learner in the classroom. Tell students that you will conduct the exercise again the next time the students give class presentations. Challenge them to improve the tally.

Advocate Appreciation of Differences

You have entered the teaching profession at a time when classrooms reflect great diversity. The rich possibilities you will encounter also come with considerable challenges.

In many schools, students with special needs work alongside general education students, creating classrooms where ability levels vary tremendously. In addition, global mobility unites students of diverse ethnic, geographic and cultural backgrounds. Family structures and lifestyles also vary. Diversity can truly enrich learning when students see each classmate as a resource, a unique person with interesting customs, talents and experiences to share with the class. Part of your role as a community builder means helping students see how much they can learn and contribute by sharing these "gifts" within a diverse community.

Encourage students to look for the unique gift each student brings to the classroom. Point out that you cannot know very much about others without talking to them and developing positive relationships with them. Challenge students to expand their friendships by taking one of the following pledges:

6

- I will try to get to know a person with whom I have not been friendly.

- I will eat lunch with someone with whom I have argued.

- I will choose someone who is different from me and try to get to know the person better.

As you teach students to deepen their appreciation for each other, reinforce the message by relating diversity to your lesson content. You may be surprised at how many opportunities you find to teach this social skill while meeting the goals of your curriculum. Social studies, language arts, art and even science and math present opportunities to help students to appreciate diversity. Consider the following examples and adapt these concepts to your own lesson plans.

Activity Idea:
No Two Alike

This activity will help you teach the concept of appreciation of differences to students as young as kindergartners.

- Begin with a discussion of snow. Explain that no two snowflakes are alike. Each one, if you could see it up close, would look like a different pattern. (Define pattern.)

- Draw some snowflakes on the board. Have students fold white paper in half, then in quarters. Show them how to cut designs in the paper, then unfold it to make a snowflake.

- Display all the snowflakes on a bulletin board. Ask students to notice how each one looks a little different. Have them point out some differences.

- Explain that children are all different, just like snowflakes. Some children like chocolate ice cream. Some like strawberry. Some can color especially well. Others can dance or sing. Ask students to notice how beautiful the snowflakes look when they are all together on the board. Point out that all children are beautiful because of their differences. We can look for ways in which each person is different and, therefore, special.

Kids Are Different

Kids are diff'rent
We don't even look the same
Some kids speak diff'rent languages
We all have a different name
Kids are different
But if you look inside you'll see
That tall kid, that small kid
Is just like you and me.
Some folks are surprised that
Kids in wheelchairs play
Blind kids read, deaf kids talk
Except in a diff'rent way.
Able kids, disabled kids
There's nothing we can't do
Just take a look inside yourself
You'll be so proud of you
Because
Kids are diff'rent
We don't even look the same
Some kids speak diff'rent languages
We all have a different name.
Kids are diff'rent
But if you look inside you'll see
That tall kid, that small kid
That deaf kid, that blind kid
Are just like you and me.

From "Kids on the Block." Lyrics by Barbara Aiello.
Permission to reprint granted to all who wish to reproduce the words to this song.

Kids Are Different
Page 224

- You may want to take Polaroid pictures of the students and place the face of each student in the snowflake he or she created.

- Reinforce the activity by reading the song lyrics "Kids Are Different" in the resource section. If you have a parent program coming up, you may want to ask parents to help each student memorize one line. For the presentation, line up the students and have them recite their lines in order.

Activity Idea:
Our Family Tree

Help students appreciate both the uniqueness and the similarities among their families.

- Create a bulletin board with a tall paper tree with a branch for each student in the room.

- Give students several squares of colored paper and let them cut out a leaf for each member of their family.

- Students write each name on a leaf and "attach" the leaves to their branch. (If they have small families, they can add names of extended family members or pets to flesh out their branch.)

- Start a family scrapbook for the whole class. Have students write about family customs, lessons family members taught them or their favorite things about each family member. (Point out that families can include step-parents, siblings, guardians, caregivers, "adopted" grandparents, etc.) Let students add drawings or photos of family members to the book.

- Let students look at the book at their leisure. Conduct a discussion about the similarities and differences among families.

Variation for older students:

- Have students meet in small groups and discuss questions such as:

  — What do you like best about your family?

  — How do you feel about the place where you live?

  — Name one thing you value in your life.

- After students have each responded to these discussions, walk around the room so you can hear the thrust of their remarks.

- Debrief the activity by asking whether some students discovered similarities or differences they had not anticipated during the discussions. Discuss how differences help people learn by hearing new perspectives.

- Ask students to meet again in their groups and find similarities and differences in their life experience or feelings. Ask them to write or tell what they learned to appreciate about the diverse members of their groups through their discussions.

6

Activity Idea:
Human Relations Stations

This activity can help teach students not to judge by appearances but to look for deeper human connections.

- Create several "stations" in the room, such as a Pet Station, Sports Station, Music Station, Hobbies Station, Family Station, Vacation Station, and Food Station. Students will evaluate their similarities and differences at stations of their choice. For older students, you might want to add stations that encourage them to delve more deeply, such as a Fear Station, Pet Peeve Station, Belief Station and Future Career Station.

- Write the names of the stations on the board and ask students to choose which three they will visit. Have students prepare a blank sheet of paper to take along. They should divide the page into two columns marked "How we're the same" and "How we're different."

- Allow students a few minutes at each of three stations. At each one, two students pair up and hold personal discussions about the topic to find at least one common experience or similar feeling and at least one difference. They write down the similarities and differences.

  For similarities, they might write, "We both want a horse but cannot have one," or "We both like swimming more than we like baseball" or "We both enjoy being the oldest child in our families," or "We both fear a bully in our neighborhood."

  For differences, they might write, "I enjoy rap music but he prefers pop music," or "She wants to be an astronaut and I want to be an artist," or "She likes to go to the mountains and I prefer the city," or "I celebrate Hanukkah and she celebrates Christmas."

- Ask students to return to their seats. In a class discussion, ask:

  — Do you feel that you know your classmates better than you did before?

  — Did you find similarities that surprised you?

  — Did you find differences that surprised you?

  — What did you learn about people? (Elicit the response that because we are all human, we are alike in as many ways as we are different.)

  — How are your differences positive?

  — What would happen if we were alike in every way?

  — What would happen if we were different in every way?

  Through this discussion, foster an awareness that we are all alike in many ways and different in many ways. Generate an understanding that human differences enrich the world yet our similarities can give us empathy for each other.

6

Teach Anger Management

Helping students learn anger management will prevent many classroom conflicts. Often the first priority in dealing with an angry student is to stop the behavior, especially when a student presents a physical danger to others. See Chapter 2, "How to Manage Behavior," for strategies to use under these circumstances. Meanwhile, keep in mind the overall goal—to help students *prevent* conflicts by controlling their own anger *before* a circumstance becomes extreme. You can keep peace in your classroom by taking time to teach students to proactively control their anger.

Teachers have used deep breathing exercises, mental exercises and other means to do this. Follow the steps below to teach your students to think before acting. Use the reproducible worksheet "Stop, Think and Act Problem-Solving Chart" in the resource section.

Stop, Think and Act
Problem-Solving Chart
Page 225

Activity Idea:
Stop, Think and Act

1. Write the word "anger" in large letters on a piece of paper. Tape it or tack it on the board and place a blank sheet of paper over it before class begins.

2. Tell students that underneath the paper lies a word representing something they must control. Ask for ideas on how to control it. Point out that until we identify what something is, we cannot control or manage it.

3. Expose the paper with the word "anger" and explain that anger management is a very important skill. Define anger management as the ability to recognize negative feelings without acting on them—to think about the actions we might take and imagine the natural consequences of our choices.

4. Point out the signs of anger, such as feeling your heart race or your face flush or your stomach tighten. Introduce the idea that when we feel anger coming on, we can do three things:

   - **Stop.** Take a few minutes to breathe deeply, count to ten and calm down.

   - **Think.** Ask yourself what is happening and why you feel angry. Think of three things you could do about it. Think about whether these actions would hurt you or someone else. Think about what would happen as a result of your decision.

   - **Act.** Choose the best plan and put it into action.

Continued on next page

Continued from previous page

5. Ask students to describe situations in which they may suddenly become angry. Use examples such as the following:

   - You are working on an art project in a group. You lay your paint brush down for a few seconds and another person takes it. You feel yourself getting angry. What will you do?

   - You feel jealous because your friend got the leading role in a play. You want to say something mean to her to show her she's not so great. What will you do?

   - You lost your homework on the way to school and the teacher gave you an "incomplete" grade. You feel very angry because you tried hard to do a good job on the homework. What will you do?

6. Distribute the problem-solving chart to everyone. Ask for a volunteer to act out one of the scenarios. At the moment of anger, instruct the student to freeze. Ask the other students to write down what thoughts the person could think that might help him or her choose the right action. When most students have finished writing, list some of their options on the board and vote on the best one.

7. Let the student finish role-playing the scenario based on the class's input. Ask students what might have happened if the student had not stopped and listened to these rational thoughts.

8. Distribute blank copies of the chart. Encourage students to keep a copy of the chart in their desks to use when they feel anger coming on.

Occasionally, you might hand a chart to a student who seems angry. In the time it takes to stop, look at the chart and think about or write down the options, the student will probably calm down. You may also want to demonstrate a special signal you will give when you want to remind a student to stop, think and act.

6

Encourage Negotiation

Managing their anger helps students avoid outbursts, but anger management alone cannot help them correct the situation making them angry. As students learn negotiation skills, they can work out a problem before it causes hurt feelings, a fight, or impaired relationships within your classroom community. You can help students of every age develop a strategy for negotiating with another person and finding solutions that satisfy everyone involved. Dr. David Johnson has explored effective ways that students can negotiate conflicts. He outlined the steps listed below. Record these steps on the board before introducing the following lesson.

Activity Idea:
A Negotiation Plan

1. Ask students if they know what it means to negotiate. Give an example from a recent history or literature lesson or from personal experience.

2. Tell students you will offer them steps for negotiating a conflict. Verbally introduce the steps below that you have listed on the board. Use the following scenario or one of your choosing to demonstrate how students can use the formula.

Sample Scenario:

Two friends meet at recess. Anna wants to sit on the grass and talk, while Kim wants to join a ball game in progress.

Anna feels that Kim must not like her or she would not want to go off and play ball. Kim thinks that Anna does not want to talk with her and is acting selfishly.

What might Anna and Kim do. *(Allow several responses.)*

You've offered some good ideas for what Kim and Anna might do. Let's see if your ideas included these negotiation steps.

Step 1: Say what you want. Problem solving requires each person to describe what he or she wants.

Anna might say, "I want you to sit and talk with me."

Kim might say, "I want you to come and play ball with me and the others."

Step 2: Say how you feel. When you hold negative feelings inside, they come back later. If you can learn to talk about your feelings in a way that does not hurt others, they might help you find solutions that help both of you.

Anna might say, "I feel lonely and hurt when you don't want to talk with me. It makes me feel that you don't want to be my friend."

Kim might say, "I feel fidgety when I've been sitting all day and you want to sit some more. It makes me angry to waste recess time."

Step 3: State your reasons. Try to understand each other's feelings by seeing the reason for the feeling.

Continued on next page

Continued from previous page

Anna might say, "Something sad happened in my family. My dad and mom had a fight. I wanted to talk about it with somebody."

Kim might say, "When I sit too long, I get bored. I need to move around or I can't think about my schoolwork."

Step 4: Reverse roles. State the other person's wishes, feelings and reasons. Make sure you understand each other by repeating what you heard the other person say.

Kim might say, "You had a bad thing happen and you need a friend to talk to."

Anna might say, "You think you won't be able to study later unless you play ball now."

Step 5: Find at least three good solutions. Think of several ways to solve the problem. Discuss which one best meets the needs of everyone involved and helps keep the friendship in place.

Kim and Anna might consider: 1) Talking for a few minutes and then playing ball; 2) playing ball at recess and walking home from school together so they could talk longer; 3) Talking as they jump rope, to get some exercise.

Step 6: Choose the best option together. Pick your solution, make a plan and shake on it.

Anna and Kim would probably choose their second solution, because Anna would have more time to express her concerns after school and could talk more easily without jumping rope at the same time. Kim would get her exercise, be able to focus on her school work, and would be a better listener for Anna after school.

Let's Talk It Out
Page 226

3. Give students copies of the "Let's Talk It Out" worksheet provided in the resource section. Ask for volunteers to role-play a problem they might invent or one they might have experienced with another student. Have the other students use the worksheet to write down notes as they complete the exercise.

4. Make blank copies of the worksheet readily available in the classroom. Invite students to use it as a tool to resolve conflicts on their own. If your students are too young to do so, have them come to you or to an aide for coaching in the steps of negotiation. Keep the steps written in a corner of the chalkboard for easy reference.

Reinforce Social Skills Through Classroom Activities

If you have read the previous parts of this chapter, you have reflected upon how you model social skills, teach them through formal presentation, and apply them in your classroom. Now look for opportunities to reinforce the social skills you have taught throughout the year. You can do this in many ways. Here are just a few.

- Have students role-play social skills that relate to a particular activity. For instance, you may need to introduce a group project in which students must share science equipment. Before proceeding, ask students to pair up and role-play an aspect of community building as it relates to group work in the science lab. Students might practice sharing space and materials, offering to clean the equipment for each other, listening to the other person's input before reporting data and complimenting the partner on his or her contribution to the work.

- At every opportunity, look for ways to relate the social skills learned to classroom interactions. When students line up for lunch, play in the schoolyard or conduct group work, watch for and point out good social skills.

- Create a bulletin board to reinforce the social skills students learned. Use the following lesson idea to make the most of the bulletin board.

Activity Idea:
Classroom Community Helpers

Look at the graphic on the next page and construct a similar bulletin board, incorporating any social skills you have taught in class. Place the center circle and some or all of the main squares on the bulletin board. Students will add the shaded items in the course of the following activity.

- Review the behaviors studied and explain that each one helps students to get along with others.

- Pair students and ask them to list sentences or phrases that indicate what each behavior looks or sounds like. For instance, "Appreciate one another's differences" might involve taking an interest in someone's family and hobbies. Students might write, "Ask about family and hobbies" on their list.

- Ask each pair of students to choose two good ideas from their list and write them on smaller pieces of construction paper.

- Place the smaller pieces around the diagram and review all the ideas.

Ask students to pick one item each week and look for an opportunity to try it. Remind them to notice when others act kind or helpful and report their observations during a class meeting or community circle.

When the bulletin board is complete, spend a portion of each day letting students study the board and tell about someone they saw acting as a community helper. Make it an honor to serve the community.

6

Classroom Community Bulletin Board

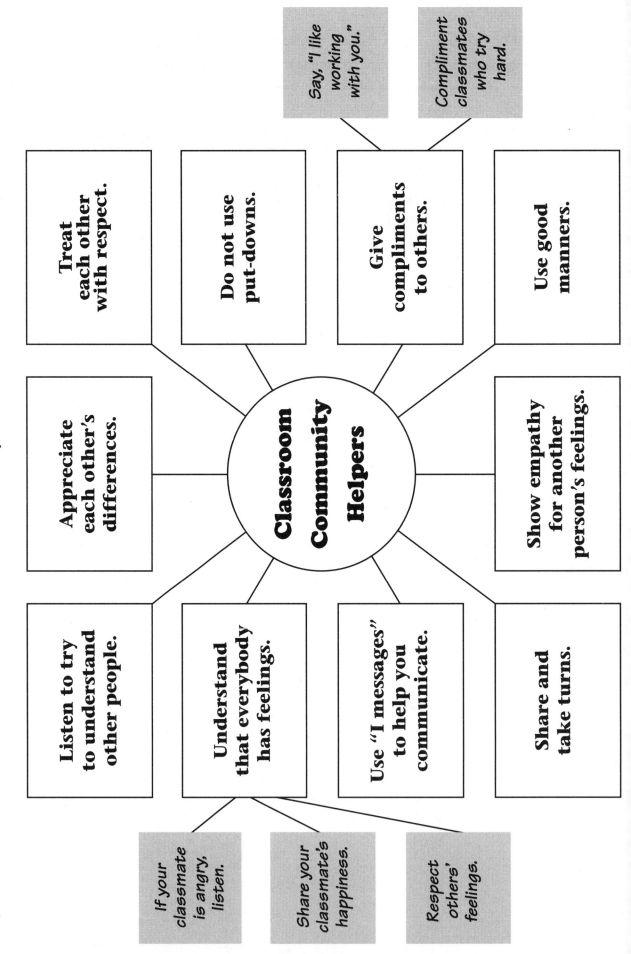

Treat each other with respect.

Do not use put-downs.

Give compliments to others.

Say, "I like working with you."

Compliment classmates who try hard.

Use good manners.

Appreciate each other's differences.

Classroom Community Helpers

Show empathy for another person's feelings.

Listen to try to understand other people.

Understand that everybody has feelings.

Use "I messages" to help you communicate.

Share and take turns.

If your classmate is angry, listen.

Share your classmate's happiness.

Respect others' feelings.

Reinforce Social Skills Through Content

Whatever your grade level or subject, you can find ways to raise students' awareness of the importance of social skills as you teach academic skills and lesson content. This section will offer ideas to serve as springboards.

Find Lessons in Literature

Reading classic literature in class provides an opportunity to introduce concepts from history and culture. It can also convey messages about human interaction. Children's poetry and fables, especially, use fantasy and metaphor to teach social skills. When you or your students read aloud, take the time to discuss the attitudes, attributes and interpersonal skills evidenced in the poem or story. To make the most of this opportunity:

- Check your school library for books of poetry and fables appropriate for your students' grade level. Select a few to read aloud in class. Facilitate a class discussion of the social skills the poems describe.

- Have students illustrate the poems and write a note about the character traits the poems discussed. Display the illustrated poems on the bulletin board.

- Have students write or dictate their own poems about social skills or character traits they think are important. Display these poems alongside the others.

Customize Your Course Content

Students' abstract thinking skills increase during the middle-school years. If you teach this age group, encourage students to begin reflecting on their lesson content to look for the messages about civic values and social interaction that history, literature and science can offer. Try the following ideas to enhance social awareness as you teach various topics across your curriculum.

Social Studies/History

Discuss with the class how cooperation or the lack of it has influenced various periods in history. Solicit students' ideas on the relationship of cooperation and conflict. Have them follow up by writing two paragraphs on one of the following topics:

- Describe a conflict that occurred in a country or period the class has studied. Did the groups participating in the conflict value cooperation? Explain how a greater or lesser level of cooperation could have changed the outcome for the country or people involved.

- Describe an historical character from your current unit of study. Did the person's character, cooperation or conflict resolution skills influence historical events? If so, how? How might the events have happened differently if the person had behaved differently?

6

Language Arts

Take the following steps or use the bullet points most appropriate for your students to teach social skills through language arts.

- Ask students whether a book or poem ever changed the way they felt about something. Ask whether they ever changed their beliefs or actions based on what they read. (They may have seen human suffering in a new light, or developed new thoughts about loyalty in friendships or about the consequences of treating people with kindness as opposed to mean-spiritedness.)

- Facilitate a discussion on the role of writers in helping shape social values and customs, for good or for bad. Ask for examples. Elicit the realization that writers help us think about our beliefs and habits and can help people reflect on the social skills they want to develop.

- Have students read quotations by famous writers and public figures and write commentaries or essays to define their own sense of the importance of certain character traits and social skills.

Science

Middle school and high school teachers in specialized subjects can find creative ways to emphasize social skills as they relate to curriculum. If you teach science, take the following steps:

- Discuss the assumption that people need social skills only in social situations. Point out that many aspects of life and work call for social skills. Ask students why they think scientists and researchers might need social skills. Elicit several responses.

- Point out that scientist learn by observing the work of others, discussing new ideas, and teaming up to find increasingly clearer answers or better solutions to a problem. They need to exercise good listening skills, speak courteously and, most of all, respect one another's ideas—even when they don't agree.

- Explain that many great advances in scientific or mathematical research came as a result of teamwork. Have students brainstorm the social skills they will need to conduct their in-class science projects.

Reinforce Social Skills Through Presentations

Several times during the year, most teachers need to coordinate student performances. You can reinforce the social skills you have taught by using them as thematic elements in class presentations. Open houses, concerts, parent appreciation nights and in-school assemblies or events present ideal opportunities to celebrate and reinforce students' understanding of the application of social skills. Students often learn on a deeper level when they create their own scripts, art work or lyrics. Add the following suggestions to your own list of ideas for reinforcing social skills through artistic presentations.

Prior to an open house or classroom event, ask students to work in small groups to plan diverse demonstrations or performances such as:

- A skit or role-play in which students demonstrate how to give and receive compliments.

- A mural showing what the world would look like if everyone exercised anger management. (Begin by discussing specific examples of how anger affects family life, schoolyard activities, interactions in stores and on busses and elsewhere in the community.)

- A student-written rap song about good manners.

- A chart showing the steps of negotiation.

- An audience reaction team to encourage good listening.

  1. Team members tell the audience the signs of good listening and encourage them to practice these skills throughout the performances.

  2. Team members hold up signs cueing the audience to "applaud," "laugh" or "listen."

  3. At the end of the performance, students applaud the audience for exhibiting listening skills.

- A puppet show about empathy or appreciation of diversity. Students can write or ad lib the script. They can make puppets using socks. For a stage, they can hang an old sheet in one corner of the classroom and cut holes at waist level. If they write the script out, pin it to the back of the sheet. The actors stand behind the sheet and put their hands through the holes and perform the action as they speak.

- A musical performance. Select familiar songs and have groups of students write new lyrics about the social skills they have learned.

6

Activity Idea:
Character Fair

Upper elementary school or middle school students may enjoy putting on a "Character Fair." This activity can help students see the importance of social skills and character development in influencing history. Plan the fair as the theme for an open house or program for parents.

• Have students impersonate historical figures who exhibited positive character traits. Students can dress in costumes and wear name tags to indicate which identity each student will take on. Cut out the character assignments on the reproducible "Characters with Character" in the resource section.

• As students greet the guests, introduce themselves and engage in conversation, guests try to guess what social skill or trait the character is demonstrating. See the reproducible on page 227 for more detailed instructions.

Characters with Character

Instructions to the teacher:

1. Make two or more copies of the reproducible character cards on pages 216 and 217. Cut out a name and identity for each student. You may have more than one student with the same identity. You may also add historical figures that relate to your content.

2. Assign each student a character to portray at the character fair. Explain that these historical figures had many talents, but their social skills and character traits helped them to influence history.

3. Students may conduct library research to find out more about their assigned characters. They can check hardcover or online encyclopedias, or you can ask them to read biographies on the individuals as an extra-credit assignment. Remind them to look at photos or illustrations to gather information that will help them create a simple costume.

4. On the day of the fair, each student will wear the costume, cut out a clean copy of the name tag, and pin it on. Students will keep the bottom portion hidden in their pockets or tucked into their costumes.

5. Students greet the guests as they arrive and initiate conversations with them. Instruct the guests to ask questions about the lives and accomplishments of the characters as they try to guess what quality the character is demonstrating.

6. Students should stay in character and exaggerate the social skill or character trait they are trying to portray. For example, if the quality is manners, the character might say "please" and "thank you" a lot. To exhibit negotiation skills, they might offer to help the guest resolve a problem.

7. After a guest has spent a few minutes trying to guess the quality, the student may read or recite the description of his or her character, revealing the special character trait.

Florence Nightingale	Harriet Tubman
Florence Nightingale: A civil war nurse who showed **helpfulness** even under the most dangerous conditions.	Harriet Tubman: This woman used her **cooperation** skills to work with others to free Southern slaves.
Eli___th Fry	**Martin Luther King**
___an went into the ___w **empathy** for the ___he taught.	Martin Luther King: This Civil Rights leader believed that people should **respect** one another despite their differences.
s Gandhi	**Albert Schweitzer**
___ leader showed the ___**manage their** ___man rights through	Albert Schweitzer: This physician felt grateful for what he had and wanted to show **kindness** to people less privileged than he was.
Keller	**Abraham Lincoln**
___ercome her inability ___nd became known for	Abraham Lincoln: This President of the United States tried to practice **fairness** by recognizing the rights of others.

Characters with Character
Page 227–229

Teaching My Students to Get Along

Before writing on the assessment form, make copies and use this assessment tool periodically during the school year. Complete the assessment to determine areas in which you are now utilizing effective skills and those in which you need to improve. Consult this book to address the areas in which you most need to focus.

Read each statement and check the appropriate response.

	Consistently	Sometimes	Seldom
1. I establish clear social expectations in my classroom.	☐	☐	☐
2. I develop age-appropriate lessons to teach my students social skills and expectations.	☐	☐	☐
3. I plan activities to increase students' ability to choose social behaviors such as listening, giving compliments, showing empathy, and treating others with respect.	☐	☐	☐
4. I develop a sense of community within my classroom.	☐	☐	☐
5. I use modeling techniques and teachable moments to reinforce social skills.	☐	☐	☐
6. I integrate social skills training into my academic curriculum.	☐	☐	☐
7. I conduct class meetings or private conversations to help students resolve problems when necessary.	☐	☐	☐
8. I assign cooperative-group activities that help students learn to get along.	☐	☐	☐
9. I teach students how to recognize and positively manage their anger.	☐	☐	☐
10. I teach students negotiation skills to encourage them to resolve conflicts on their own.	☐	☐	☐
11. I assess the effectiveness of my efforts and make follow-up plans.	☐	☐	☐

Getting Along in School

To do your best work in school, you need to feel safe and you need to get along with other students. Please answer each question honestly. You don't have to put your name on the paper.

1. I think most students in this class get along with each other.   Yes   No

   If no, why do you think so? _____

2. I think most students in this school get along with each other.   Yes   No

   If no, why do you think so? _____

3. I have been teased by students in my class.   Yes   No

   If yes, where? _____

   How often (such as once in a while, every week, every day)? _____

4. I have been teased by students in other classes.   Yes   No

   If yes, where? _____

   How often (such as once in a while, every week, every day)? _____

5. I have been in fights that involved shouting or name-calling.   Yes   No

   If yes, where? _____

   How often (such as once in a while, every week, every day)? _____

   With students in my class? _____

   With students in other classes? _____

6. I have seen fights that involved hitting or hurting.   Yes   No

   If yes, where? _____

   How often (such as once in a while, every week, every day)? _____

   Among students in my class? _____

   Among students in other classes? _____

Good Manners
Word Puzzle

R	E	S	U	C	G	G	R	P	E	N	D	U
E	R	O	P	I	I	R	S	O	P	R	U	M
C	E	C	P	U	S	E	A	L	O	M	C	A
T	F	I	L	O	I	E	Z	C	L	A	O	N
C	I	E	E	S	L	T	G	I	I	N	N	N
I	N	T	A	C	T	I	R	T	T	O	D	E
C	E	Y	S	O	T	N	A	R	E	S	U	R
U	D	R	E	R	E	G	A	R	D	Y	C	S
L	C	E	V	D	R	E	S	P	E	C	T	E
T	O	F	C	I	V	I	L	I	T	Y	C	P
U	U	I	T	A	I	N	E	C	I	O	U	S
R	R	W	E	L	C	O	M	E	E	O	U	S
E	C	O	U	R	T	E	O	U	S	A	R	G

Find These Words:

POLITE	RESPECT	CULTURE	PLEASE
COURTEOUS	CIVILITY	TACT	GRACIOUS
MANNERS	REGARD	CORDIAL	REFINED
GREETING	WELCOME	SOCIETY	CONDUCT

Name: _____

Good Manners
Comic Strip

1	2
3	4

Catalog of Compliments

I like you.

You look nice.

I'm glad we're friends.

I like working with you.

You're fun.

I'd like to get to know you better.

You're a good buddy.

Congratulations for…

Thank you for sharing…

I like the way you look.

You're super at…

I'm glad we're friends.

I wish you a wonderful day.

Thank you for teaching me something new today.

I appreciate your help.

Thanks for including me.

You are a kind person.

You're funny.

It's nice to see you in school every day.

You are dependable.

You're a great listener.

You are very creative.

I like it when you…

I'm happy to know you.

Good job.

I'm proud of you because…

You are special…

I like it when you smile…

You're my special friend.

I'm glad you are in our class.

You are a caring person.

You are very helpful.

I enjoy being with you.

How nice of you to do that.

I think you are terrific.

I hope you do well. You deserve it.

You give the best compliments.

I especially appreciated it when you…

I'm glad you're in my group.

You're fun to know.

Your clothes look great!

I feel good when I'm with you.

You made me laugh.

I like to sit with you.

You are a great friend.

I like playing with you.

You're a good buddy.

I like your…

I'm glad I know you.

You are so smart.

I like the way you…

You're easy to get along with.

You are a great helper.

I appreciate your help.

You're so good in sports.

You're the best!

To: _____

From: _____

You Deserve a Compliment!

To: _____

From: _____

You Deserve a Compliment!

To: _____

From: _____

You Deserve a Compliment!

To: _____

From: _____

You Deserve a Compliment!

Checklist of Good Listening Skills

As you monitor the quality of the listening, check the answer that best applies.

	Often	Sometimes	Never
Voice:			
Good listeners do not interrupt, except to ask questions.	☐	☐	☐
Good listeners repeat back what the speaker said.	☐	☐	☐
Eyes:			
Good listeners look at the speaker's eyes.	☐	☐	☐
Head:			
Good listeners turn toward the speaker.	☐	☐	☐
Ears:			
Good listeners filter out other distractions.	☐	☐	☐
Mind:			
Good listeners think about the speaker's message.	☐	☐	☐

Checklist of Good Listening Skills

As you monitor the quality of the listening, check the answer that best applies.

	Often	Sometimes	Never
Voice:			
Good listeners do not interrupt, except to ask questions.	☐	☐	☐
Good listeners repeat back what the speaker said.	☐	☐	☐
Eyes:			
Good listeners look at the speaker's eyes.	☐	☐	☐
Head:			
Good listeners turn toward the speaker.	☐	☐	☐
Ears:			
Good listeners filter out other distractions.	☐	☐	☐
Mind:			
Good listeners think about the speaker's message.	☐	☐	☐

Kids Are Different

Kids are diff'rent
We don't even look the same
Some kids speak diff'rent languages
We all have a different name
Kids are different
But if you look inside you'll see
That tall kid, that small kid
Is just like you and me.
Some folks are surprised that
Kids in wheelchairs play
Blind kids read, deaf kids talk
Except in a diff'rent way.
Able kids, disabled kids
There's nothing we can't do
Just take a look inside yourself
You'll be so proud of you
Because
Kids are diff'rent
We don't even look the same
Some kids speak diff'rent languages
We all have a different name.
Kids are diff'rent
But if you look inside you'll see
That tall kid, that small kid
That deaf kid, that blind kid
Are just like you and me.

From "Kids on the Block." Lyrics by Barbara Aiello.
Permission to reprint granted to all who wish to reproduce the words to this song.

Stop, Think and Act
Problem-Solving Chart

Name the problem. _____

Stop! Take a few moments to calm down.

Think! First think of three actions you could take. Write them down.
Then ask yourself these questions about each action.

Action 1:

                                                Yes   No

_____ Will this action hurt me? ☐ ☐

_____ Will this action hurt others? ☐ ☐

_____ Will this action resolve the problem? ☐ ☐

Action 2:

_____ Will this action hurt me? ☐ ☐

_____ Will this action hurt others? ☐ ☐

_____ Will this action resolve the problem? ☐ ☐

Action 3:

_____ Will this action hurt me? ☐ ☐

_____ Will this action hurt others? ☐ ☐

_____ Will this action resolve the problem? ☐ ☐

Act! What will I choose to do? Write down the best action, then do it.

_____

_____

_____

Let's Talk It Out

When you have a problem, don't *take* it out *on* someone. *Talk* it out *with* someone. Sit down with the person you are having the problem with and follow these steps:

- Talk about the problem. Say what you want.
- Say how you feel.
- Tell why you feel that way.
- See the situation from the other person's eyes. Pretending you are that person, tell your wishes, feelings and reasons.
- Together, come up with three ideas that will solve the problem and make you both feel better. Pick the best solution.
- Shake on it!

Possible solutions

1. _____

_____

_____

2. _____

_____

_____

3. _____

_____

_____

Best solution

_____

_____

That's a great solution!

_____

_____

Characters with Character

Instructions to the teacher:

1. Make two or more copies of the reproducible character cards on pages 228 and 229. Cut out a name and identity for each student. You may have more than one student with the same identity. You may also add historical figures that relate to your content.

2. Assign each student a character to portray at the character fair. Explain that these historical figures had many talents, but their social skills and character traits helped them to influence history.

3. Students may conduct library research to find out more about their assigned characters. They can check hard-cover or online encyclopedias, or you can ask them to read biographies on the individuals as an extra-credit assignment. Remind them to look at photos or illustrations to gather information that will help them create a simple costume.

4. On the day of the fair, each student will wear the costume, cut out a clean copy of the name tag, and pin it on. Students will keep the bottom portion hidden in their pockets or tucked into their costumes.

5. Students greet the guests as they arrive and initiate conversations with them. Instruct the guests to ask questions about the lives and accomplishments of the characters as they try to guess what quality the character is demonstrating.

6. Students should stay in character and exaggerate the social skill or character trait they are trying to portray. For example, if the quality is manners, the character might say "please" and "thank you" a lot. To exhibit negotiation skills, they might offer to help the guest resolve a problem.

7. After a guest has spent a few minutes trying to guess the quality, the student may read or recite the description of his or her character, revealing the special character trait.

Florence Nightingale

Florence Nightingale: A civil war nurse who showed **helpfulness** even under the most dangerous conditions.

Harriet Tubman

Harriet Tubman: This woman used her **cooperation** skills to work with others to free Southern slaves.

Elizabeth Fry

Elizabeth Fry: This woman went into the prisons of London to show **empathy** for the poor female prisoners she taught.

Martin Luther King

Martin Luther King: This Civil Rights leader believed that people should **respect** one another despite their differences.

Mohandas Gandhi

Mohandas Gandhi: This leader showed the people of India how to **manage their anger** and work for human rights through peaceful means.

Albert Schweitzer

Albert Schweitzer: This physician felt grateful for what he had and wanted to show **kindness** to people less privileged than he was.

Helen Keller

Helen Keller: This girl overcame her inability to see, speak or hear and became known for her refined **manners.**

Abraham Lincoln

Abraham Lincoln: This President of the United States tried to practice **fairness** by recognizing the rights of others.

Sacajewea

Sacajewea: This young Indian scout led Lewis and Clark to the Pacific Ocean. She used her **peacemaking skills** to establish relationships between the explorers and her people.

Charles Dickens

Charles Dickens: This author improved child labor laws by listening carefully to the problems of others and turning them into stories. He had **empathy** for the problems of others.

John Jay

As the first U.S. Supreme Court Judge, John Jay had the task of working in a group to understand and resolve conflicts. His leadership exhibited his **conflict resolution skills.**

Carl Jung

Carl Jung: This man used his **listening skills** to try to understand people. His ideas and counseling style helped to shape the field called psychoanalysis.

Woodrow Wilson

Woodrow Wilson: This U.S. President exercised his **negotiation skills** by inviting other nations to join in a League of Nations to preserve peace.

George Washington

As the first U.S. President, George Washington would not accept the title of "king." He knew that to create a democracy, he must share responsibility with others and some day pass it on. Because he valued **humility** over power, he ensured the future of the democracy.

Mark Twain

Mark Twain: This famous author often had differences of opinion with co-workers or family members. He learned the value of **apologizing** and trying to correct the situations he had created.

Cesar Chavez

Cesar Chavez: This labor organizer believed in **treating others fairly.** He led a non-violent struggle to improve the lives and restore the dignity of mistreated farm workers.

CHAPTER 7

How to Ensure Personal and Professional Growth

" It helps to say if something isn't working. In the teacher's lounge, in between classes—everybody just brainstorms about what is working and is not working. There's a real camaraderie. I guess it's my support system. I couldn't have done without it this year. "

Teaching is more an art than a science, more a process than a practice. Throughout your teaching career, you will find more than one effective way to accomplish a goal, and what works best in your first year of teaching may not feel right in your second, third or fourth year. Your success and satisfaction will depend on your ability to evolve along with your students.

You could have chosen any career. But you chose to hone young minds and lives. The complex human variables that reshape your class from year to year and from day to day will keep your job from becoming static or boring—or easy! Effective teachers expect to pursue a professional path equally as dynamic, challenging and fluid as their changing classrooms. Commit to continued growth as a teacher and you will magnify your students' potential along with your own.

As you face the challenges of first-year teaching, save time to refresh and reflect. Here you will find tips for recharging your internal battery as well as plugging yourself into the system. You will also see resource lists to keep and consider as you move along your professional path. Remember, one mark of a first-class teacher is the commitment to live life as a continual learner.

Become a Lifelong Learner

You may have heard the term "lifelong learners" as it relates to your students. The same principle of lifelong learning applies to your career. Because you care about the children in your charge, you will continually strive to create an effective learning environment for them. Remember to nurture your own growth at the same time.

Reflect on Your Experience

Develop the habit of reflecting on your teaching practices. Analyze how you present curriculum and how you relate with students. Reflect on your positive and negative experiences, your successes and your failures. Become a student as you continually refine your approach to teaching. The following self-test outlines the qualities of a successful classroom. Check off the items in which you feel you need improvement, and seek strategies to make next year better.

___ **Modeling self-discipline.** I am well prepared for class, on time, and organized. Even if I get angry, I show students respect.

___ **Clarity of expectations.** Limits and consequences for behavior are clear. Students have individual learning goals.

___ **Consistency.** Rules are enforced equally for all students.

___ **Student safety.** Students feel secure and free from threat in my classroom.

___ **Caring.** I greet students and ask about their interests. I have individual conferences with students who are having problems in class.

___ **Teamwork.** I emphasize cooperation over competition.

___ **High quality instruction.** I use a variety of teaching strategies and tell students how a topic or skill they are learning is useful/relevant to their lives.

___ **Timing.** I maintain a brisk instructional pace and make smooth transitions between activities.

___ **Responsiveness.** I give students immediate constructive feedback. I deal with misbehavior as quickly as possible.

___ **Reinforcing good behavior.** I recognize the success, improvements and contributions of individual students.

___ **Self-discipline.** I teach students self-monitoring skills.

___ **Parent involvement.** I enlist parents' help and show them how to contribute to their children's education.

Source: Excerpted from the Teacher Institute; published in *Better Teaching,* June 19, 1998.

Surround Yourself with Professionals

You can gain a more global perspective and still find like-minded role models by reaching out into the professional community. Join organizations. Attend conventions. These gatherings often motivate teachers to further their exploration of developments in education and study new topics of interest or areas of specific need. Most teachers come away from conventions not only with bags full of sample materials but with new relationships. Professional associations offer rich and often rejuvenating opportunities to share your passions and problems with other teachers.

To connect with colleagues, check the resource sheet "Professional Development Resources and Organizations." Also ask your district about regional organizations.

Professional Development Resources
and Organizations
Page 241

Learn from a Mentor

Look for a role model with the skills to "teach the teacher." Find a colleague who supports your growth, provides positive feedback and models excellent teaching practices that reflect your own philosophies. Chapter 1 described mentorship programs in which schools assign an experienced teacher to assist a new teacher in acclimating to the school community and finding materials and curriculum resources. There's no need to stop collaborating beyond your first year.

If you do not establish a bond with a mentor teacher early in your first year, continue to search for a long-term mentor. Arrange to visit several classrooms and observe other teachers in action. Talk to them about their experiences. Ask for permission to tap a teacher's brain—and sometimes lean on his or her shoulder. Invite this master teacher to observe you with your students and provide constructive feedback and reinforcement. You may also want to ask to see this teacher's professional portfolio for your own reference in creating a teaching portfolio.

Learn from Media

Even in a room full of students, you may sometimes feel isolated in your work. When you cannot talk to a colleague in person, you can always stimulate your own enthusiasm, learn new ideas and keep your teaching practice up-to-date by reading the many professional journals and books available to today's educators. Set aside a little time each week to read professional development materials. Subscribe to some of the publications listed on the resource sheet "Professional Journals," and visit their Web sites. You may also want to deepen your understanding of a particular topic by reading the books on the resource sheet "Books Recommended for New Teachers." Although a few contain in-depth theory, most have been written in a hands-on way that will help you improve your teaching practices relatively quickly. You will find both of these lists in the resource section.

Professional Journals
Page 242

Books Recommended for New Teachers
Page 243

Sharpen Your Skills and Credentials

Many excellent graduate-studies programs can help you improve your daily teaching practices and advance you along your career path. School districts offer pay increases for teachers who earn advanced degrees or graduate-credit units. Check the Web for available programs or contact a nearby university.

Schools and districts also sponsor seminars and workshops specifically designed for new teachers, so attend whenever possible. Check your district's professional development catalog or read the school announcements. Look for additional professional development opportunities on the Internet. For starters, visit the professional growth sites listed on the "Web Resources Recommended for New Teachers" sheet in the resource section.

Web Resources Recommended
for New Teachers
Page 244

Pump Up Your Portfolio

Document your own successes, just as you record student successes. Begin your own professional portfolio. You will need certain documents to establish your credentials when applying for a new job. Add materials to the file that chart your progress over this first year and throughout your career.

Your files can include:

- Your teaching certificate and an individual professional development plan.
- Transcripts of degrees and college credits, including attendance records.
- Evaluations, awards and honors, and professional organization affiliations.
- Letters of recommendation from administrators, colleagues and parents.
- Sample lesson plans and corresponding photos of completed student projects.
- Statements from students reflecting how your influence affected them or how a particular lesson or activity influenced their learning.
- A videotape of a presentation or activity you facilitated.
- Samples of individual student work showing growth over time.

Plot Your Course

Your portfolio can capture the highlights of your career, but you will also need to create a special file to keep track of the practical details and events that occur throughout the year. You may refer to this file when you need to settle a dispute with a parent, make a report to your principal or counselor, or document accommodations for students with special needs. Make sure your file includes the following:

- Letters of hire, employment contracts and any supplemental contracts you may have signed.
- Records of your salary, retirement plan, insurance plan and time off.
- Documentation of incidents involving student discipline. (See pages 62 and 63 for suggestions.)
- Records of referrals of students with special needs and documentation of any modifications in classroom routines and learning strategies made for these students.
- Copies of all correspondence from school or district administrators.
- Copies of all correspondence from parents regarding discipline or student behavior.

De-stress for Success

As a new teacher, you may quickly learn why your occupation ranks high on the list of stressful jobs. Ironically, the caring quality that makes a teacher exemplary can lead to anxiety. Awareness that the work helps chart the course of young people's lives can produce a lot of pressure. Excellence becomes imperative for a teacher who wants to make a difference.

Your colleagues may inadvertently discourage you by discussing negative factors such as lack of support from administration, work overload and apathetic parents. As the year goes on, you will probably grapple with ways to balance these anxieties and aspirations.

Your challenges will seem more manageable if you expect them and come to understand them. Stress often refers to the reaction of the body as it mobilizes its defenses against a perceived threat. In stressful situations, messages from the brain stimulate nerves and chemical reactions, which cause a rush of adrenaline, gearing your body up for action. Stress, then, exists not only in your mind but in your body. Learn to recognize your body's cues, such as changes in appetite, fatigue, frequent illness or headaches.

When you feel stress, look for opportunities to:

- Take a walk around your room or out in the schoolyard.
- Do some deep breathing exercises to relax.
- Identify the source of your stress.
- Talk to a colleague about it.

Seek the Source of Stress

Once you have dealt with the symptoms, address the sources of your stress. Do you feel worried about a challenging student or pressure from a parent or administrator? Do you wonder how to accomplish all you need to during the course of the school day? Are you concerned about meeting educational standards? Do you have bilingual students or students whose special needs keep you feeling stretched thin? Consider measures to correct the sources of stress:

- Ask your administration for a teacher's aide.
- Ask a counselor for help with difficult students.
- Re-evaluate your schedule and priorities if time pressure is a problem.
- Seek out a support group, drawing on the ideas that follow.

Avoid Isolation

As a new teacher, you may experience burnout or feel you have to bear your responsibilities alone. Talking and sharing with other teachers can help you combat that burnout. Even though you feel pressed for time, make sure your schedule allows you to collaborate and interact with colleagues. Try these suggestions:

- Ask your colleagues if any of them would like to collaborate with you on a regular basis. You may need to solicit the help of your administration to create more time for teachers to collaborate.

- When you visit the faculty lounge, use the time to develop relationships with colleagues who express enthusiasm about their teaching practices.

- See the suggestions on page 234 for surrounding yourself with professionals.

- Sign up with a formal professional organization. The involvement will help you feel less isolated and more vital and enthusiastic. If you did not find an organization of interest on page 241, ask your colleagues if they know of a support group of teachers who share your interests and job-related problems.

- Send a note to the teachers in your school, content area or grade level. Invite them to drop a note in your teacher's mailbox with any tips or "best ideas" they would like to share with you. Thank them in advance for their ideas and support.

Request Emotional Support

Support from those closest to you becomes a key ingredient in coping with occupational stress. Help your family members and friends understand that you have a demanding job and that you may need whatever free time you have just to recoup your strength to go back into your classroom the next day. Surround yourself with people who appreciate the challenges of your profession and the significance of your role in society so you will receive positive feedback and encouragement in your personal and professional life.

Keep Fit

Watch your diet and exercise regularly. Always eat breakfast, especially if your most demanding classes occur in the morning. Keeping your blood sugar and carbohydrate level up will help you to avoid becoming irritable or fatigued before lunch time.

Tackle Time Management

Many new teachers find that they have too much to do and too little time in which to do it. They feel that they have too much responsibility. They must continually adapt to new rules, regulations and policies. They know they need to acquire new teaching skills and learn new ways to deal with student behavior. These realities require strong coping and adapting skills. Managing your time effectively can give you an edge in avoiding the stress these pressures generate.

Make a habit of ordering your priorities each day. Set aside a few minutes at the end of the day to plan your priorities for the following day. Ask what you can realistically accomplish and what you can delegate, using the reproducible worksheet "Prioritize!" in the resource section. Use a monthly calendar or plan book to decide how and when to achieve the long-term goals of your curriculum.

Prioritize!

Try this daily exercise to stay focused, organized and effective.
- What are the three most important accomplishments I can make today?
- How can I best accomplish these tasks? What should I delegate to others?
- How would it affect my day if I did not achieve these accomplishments?

Three Top Priorities:

1
2
3

What I will do:

What I can delegate:

What I will do only if I have time:

Prioritize!
Page 245

Keep a Personal Journal

Your first year will offer many landmarks you will recognize in years to come—first-day challenges, student behavior issues, report card dilemmas, event stresses, pre-holiday distractions and end-of-year restlessness, to name a few. Record your challenges and solutions for future reference. When something positive happens in your classroom, make a note of it. When you discover a strategy especially suited to your style or your school, describe it. When you feel frustrated and suddenly experience a breakthrough, celebrate it in writing.

A journal can serve as a means of perpetual self-evaluation as well as a keepsake. You don't have to write in it every day or even every week. Just jot down your reflections when you feel inspired to do so. Through the process of writing, you may come to refine your values and teaching strategies and identify insights that will help you throughout the school year.

7

Postscript

In every block of marble I see a statue as plain as though it stood before me, shaped and perfect in attitude and action. I have only to hew away the rough walls that imprison the lovely apparition to reveal it to the other eyes as mine see it.

—Michelangelo

Students achieve when teachers believe. Envision and activate the potential of every student and you will empower yourself as a teacher. As you build the foundations for a fulfilling career, you will enjoy a higher privilege—to inspire a love of learning.

Through small daily acts you will fulfill a big vision. You will share ideas and foster interactions that touch a whole new generation of thinkers and doers. You will shape character as you sculpt minds.

Go out and teach, then reveal your masterpieces to the world.

Professional Development Resources and Organizations

American Federation of Teachers (AFT)
555 New Jersey Avenue, NW
Washington, DC 20001
202-879-4400

www.aft.org

AFT helps teachers at state and local levels with collective bargaining, public relations and research. Areas of research include bilingual education, teacher certification and education reform. AFT-sponsors the Learning Activities Hotline: 1-800-242-5465.

Association for Supervision and Curriculum Development (ASCD)
1703 No. Beauregard St.
Alexandria, VA 22311-1714
1-800-933-ASCD

www.ascd.org

ASCD is a membership organization for leaders in elementary, middle, and secondary education, and for anyone interested in instruction, supervision, curriculum and leadership in schools. ASCD produces a journal, newsletters, books, and training materials on topics of interest to members.

Educational Products Information Exchange (EPIE)
103 Montauk Highway
Hampton Bays, NY 11946
516-728-9100

www.interhelp.com/epieinfo.htm

This organization analyzes all types of teaching materials and provides information to schools and educators through publications, newsletters and analysis reports.

Elementary School Center
Two E. 103rd Street
New York, NY 10029
212-289-5929

This organization works to improve the quality of schooling, increase awareness of the effects of elementary schooling in children's lives, and encourage cooperation and communication among groups working with children.

National Association for Multicultural Education (NAME)
733 15th St., NW, Suite 430
Washington, D.C. 20005
202-628-6263

www.inform.umd.edu/name

This office coordinates an annual conference on multicultural education for teachers and teacher educators.

National Association for the Education of Young Children
1509 16th Street, NW
Washington, DC 20036-1426
1-800-424-2460

www.naeyc.org

An association dedicated to improving the quality of care and education for children, offering publications, training materials, and policy-related information. They administer the National Academy of Early Childhood Programs, a voluntary national accreditation system.

National Board for Professional Teaching Standards (NBPTS)
26555 Evergreen Rd., Suite 400
Southfield, MI 48076
248-351-4444

www.nbpts.org

This board's mission is to establish high standards for what accomplished teachers should know and be able to do, by developing a system of certification for teachers.

National Education Association (NEA)
1201 16th Street, NW
Washington, DC 20036
202-833-4000

www.nea.org

NEA is the nation's largest organization committed to advancing the cause of public education.

National Middle School Association (NMSA)
4151 Executive Pkwy, Suite 300
Westerville, OH 43081
1-800-528-NMSA (6672)

www.nmsa.org

This group is for teachers and others interested in middle school education as a distinct entity in American education. NMSA publishes *Middle Ground and Middle School Journal*.

U.S. Department of Education
400 Maryland Ave., SW
Washington, DC 20202
1-800-USA-LEARN

www.ed.gov/free

For quick access to hundreds of free resources, for information on national standards, policies and programs or to check for educational organizations in your area, contact the U.S. Department of Education.

Professional Journals

Creative Classroom
Children's Television Workshop
One Lincoln Plaza
New York, NY 10023

www.creativeclassroom.org

Educational Leadership
Association for Supervision and
Curriculum Development
1703 No. Beauregard St.
Alexandria, VA 22314

www.ascd.org

Education Week
Suite 100
6935 Arlington Road
Bethesda, MD 20814-5233
1-800-346-1834

www.edweek.org

Electronic Learning
Scholastic Inc.
555 Broadway
New York, NY 10012
212-343-6100

*www.scholastic.com/public/EL/
EL.html*

Instructor Magazine
Scholastic Inc.
555 Broadway
New York, NY 10012
212-343-6100

scholastic.com/Instructor

Language Arts
National Council of Teachers of
English
1111 W. Kenyon Rd.
Urbana, IL 61801-1096
1-800-369-6283

www.ncte.org

Learning
3515 W. Market St.
Suite 200
Greensboro, NC 27403
888-255-3110

www.learningmagazine.com

Phi Delta Kappan
P.O. Box 789
Bloomington, IN 47402-0789
1-800-766-1156

*www.pdkintl.org/kappan/
kappan.htm*

The Professional Educator
Auburn University
3084 Haley Center
Auburn, AL 36849-5218
334-844-5793

*www.auburn.edu/academic/
education/tpi/proedmp.htm*

Reading Teacher
International Reading Association
P.O. Box 8139
Newark, DE 19714
302-731-1600

www.reading.org

Teacher Magazine
6935 Arlington Road, Suite 100
Bethesda, MD 20814-5233
1-800-346-1834

www.teachermagazine.org

Teaching Pre K-8 Magazine
40 Richards Avenue
Norwalk, CT 06854
1-800-249-9363

www.teachingk-8.com

**Host Web sites to links
featuring additional
journals for educators:**

National Forum Journals
www.nationalforum.com

NewsDirectory.com
*www.ecola.com/news/
magazine/current/edu/*

Triangle Journals
www.triangle.co.uk/index.htm

Books Recommended for New Teachers

Assessment

Assessment in the Learning Organization: Shifting the Paradigm
A.L. Costa & B. Kallick
ASCD, 1995
Alexandria, Virginia

How to Assess Authentic Learning
K. Burke
Allyn and Bacon, 1998
Boston, Massachusetts

Portfolio Assessment: Getting Started
A. A. De Fina
Scholastic, 1996
New York, New York

Behavior Management

Assertive Discipline
L. Canter & M. Canter
Canter & Associates, 1992
Santa Monica, California

The Caring Teacher's Guide to Discipline: Helping Young Students Learn Self-Control, Responsibility and Respect
M. Gootman
Corwin, 1997
Thousand Oaks, California

Classroom Management for Elementary Teachers
C.M. Evertson, E.T. Emmer,
B.S. Clements & M.E. Worsham
Allyn and Bacon, 1999
Boston, Massachusetts

Classroom Management for Secondary Teachers
E.T. Emmer, C.M. Evertson,
B.S. Clements, & M.E. Worsham
Allyn and Bacon, 1999
Boston, Massachusetts

Rallying the Whole Village: The Comer Process for Reforming
Education
J.P. Comer, N.M. Haynes & E.T. Joyner
Teachers College Press, 1996
New York, New York

101 Ways to Develop Student Self-esteem and Responsibility
J. Canfield & F. Siccone
Allyn and Bacon, 1994
Boston, Massachusetts

Cooperative Learning

Cooperation in the Classroom
D.W. Johnson & R.T. Johnson
Interaction Book Company, 1998
Edina, Minnesota

Conflict Resolution

Creative Controversy: Intellectual Challenge in the Classroom
D.W. Johnson & R.T. Johnson
Interaction Book Company, 1995
Edina, Minnesota

Teaching Children to Be Peacemakers
D.W. Johnson & R.T. Johnson
Interaction Book Company, 1995
Edina, Minnesota

Inclusion

Including Students with Special Needs
M. Friend & W. Bursuck
Allyn and Bacon, 1996
Boston, Massachusetts

Instruction

Inspiring Active Learning
M. Harmin
Inspiring Strategy Institute, 1995
Edwardsville, Illinois

Teaching Styles and Strategies
H. Silver, R.J. Hanson,
R.W. Strong & P.B. Schwartz
The Thoughtful Education Press, 1996
Oradell, New Jersey

Literacy

Evaluating Literacy: A Perspective for Change
R.J. Anthony, T.D. Johnson, N.I. Mickelson & A. Preece
Heinemann, 1991
Portsmouth, New Hampshire

Motivating Students

Motivation To Learn: From Theory to Practice (1998)
D. Stipek
Allyn and Bacon, 1998
Boston, Massachusetts

Reaching and Teaching Every Student

Failing at Fairness: How America's Schools Cheat Girls
D. & M. Sadker
Simon & Schuster, 1994
New York, New York

Learning Styles and Strategies
J.R. Hanson & H.F. Silver
The Thoughtful Education Press, 1996
Oradell, New Jersey

Multiple Intelligences School
S. Teele
Sue Teele & Associates, 1995
Redlands, California

Multiple Intelligences: The Theory in Practice
H. Gardner
Basic Books, 1993
New York, New York

Self-Directed Learning

The School as a Home for the Mind
A. L. Costa
Skylight Press, 1991
Arlington Heights, Illinois

Technology

A Teacher's Guide to the Information Highway
W. Wresch
Merrill/Prentice Hall, 1997
Upper Saddle River, New Jersey

Web Resources
Recommended for New Teachers

Blue Web'n

www.kn.pacbell.com/wired/bluewebn

A searchable database of Internet learning sites categorized by subject area, audience and type (lessons, activities, projects, resources, references and tools). Sponsored by Pacific Bell.

Canter

www.canterweb.com

View a wide menu of graduate course descriptions and staff development materials designed to help teachers plan a course of continuing professional development.

Educational Theory

www.ed.uiuc.edu/EPS/Educational-Theory/

Deepen your understanding of the philosophy of education in the site of abstracts from journal issues.

ERIC Clearinghouse on Teaching and Teacher Education

American Association of Colleges for Teacher Education
1307 New York Ave., NW
Suite 300
Washington, D.C. 20005-2450
1-800-822-9229
or 202-293-2450

www.ericsp.org

The ultimate link for educational research. Reference and referral services and online searches; conduct training, seminars, and workshops; and produce and distribute free and low-cost publications.

Federal Resources for Educational Excellence (FREE)

www.ed.gov/free

Offers access to hundreds of teaching and learning resources across the federal government, from historical documents and scientific experiments to mathematical challenges and famous paintings. The site supports partnerships between federal agencies and teachers to develop additional resources.

From Now On

www.fno.org

Jamie MacKenzie publishes this free educational technology journal with links to policy issues, curriculum helps, and much more.

I Love Teaching.com

www.iloveteaching.com/

This site contains information devoted to encouraging teachers and potential teachers.

K–12 World

www.k-12world.com/

A collection of links to educational sites and resources.

Kathy Schrock's Guide for Educators

www.school.discovery.com/schrockguide/

A categorized list of sites useful for enhancing curriculum and professional growth. Updated daily.

Teaching Excellent Mathematics, Science and Elementary Education

www.dimacs.rutgers.edu/nti

Learn about institutes to help you teach problem solving and conceptual understanding and tap into a supportive network of peers and mentors. Geared to K–12.

TeachNet.com

www.teachnet.com/top.htm

Learn helpful advice and strategies to improve your performance.

Teachers Helping Teachers

www.pacificnet.net/~mandel/index.html

Working teachers and administrators submit helpful ideas, activities and survival strategies for new teachers.

Tenth Planet

www.tenthplanet.com/

Award-winning curriculum software and links to teacher resources.

Peak Learning Systems

www.peaklearn.com/

Resource site for education students, student teachers, first-year teachers and those interested in becoming teachers.

Virtual Schoolhouse

www.metalab.unc.edu/cisco/schoolhouse

This site features not only virtual field trips and student resources but also teaching resources and links to software archives.

For student project Web sites, see pages 157–158.

For professional organization Web sites, see page 241.

For professional journal Web sites, see page 242.

Prioritize!

Try this daily exercise to stay focused, organized and effective.

- What are the three most important accomplishments I can make today?
- How can I best accomplish these tasks? What should I delegate to others?
- How would it affect my day if I did not achieve these accomplishments?

Three Top Priorities:

1.

2.

3.

What I will do:

What I can delegate:

What I will do only if I have time:

Topical Index